KNOW
JEWISH LIVING
AND
ENJOY IT

KNOW JEWISH LIVING AND ENJOY IT

by MORRIS GOLOMB

SHENGOLD PUBLISHERS, INC.

New York City

ISBN 0-88400-054-0

Library of Congress Catalog Card Number: 78-54569

Copyright © 1981 by Morris Golomb

Published by Shengold Publishers, Inc.
New York, N.Y.

Printed in the United States of America

Dedicated to the loving memory of a young man whom we admired for his sterling character, his deep devotion and sincerity — one who learned, lived, loved, and spread the words of Torah in full measure, to ARNOLD KLEIN Z"L.

CONTENTS

INTRODUCTION

There is a legend of a man who walked through a dense London fog and saw a big dark mass looming before him. As he came closer he saw that the mass was a man like himself. When finally he was face to face with the man, he saw that it was his own long-lost brother.

This legend could serve as an analogy for the situation of many of our young Jewish people today. Stumbling through the fog of ignorance, they see the dim outlines of their Jewish heritage, but they will not be able to behold it clearly in all its beauty until the fog has lifted.

My desire to help lift the fog of ignorance that surrounds so much of our heritage has prompted me to undertake this work on Jewish customs and ceremonies. I have long felt the need for correcting many commonly held misconceptions about the observances of the Jewish religion and for presenting the laws and customs of Judaism in a manner that would be meaningful to our younger generation.

I have been encouraged by the warm and generous response which has greeted my previous work, *Know Your Festivals and Enjoy Them*, since it was published in 1973. I feel it only natural now to go on from the festivals to the business of everyday Jewish living. This new book is meant for young readers from the age of eleven or twelve onward.

I begin by describing each custom and ceremony, then discuss its background and the reasons for its observance, within the limits of our knowledge and understanding. Next, I give suggestions for spiritual benefits to be gained from them. All along, the reader is encouraged to follow up each subject with additional reading.

Our sages have said, "It is not merely the *study* of a mitzvah that counts most, but rather its *performance*" (Ethics of the Fathers 1:17).

Later scholars, however, pointed out that while practical performance was vital, the value of study is just as great if not greater because it is only through theoretical knowledge that one can arrive at the proper observance of a mitzvah.

It is hoped that, in keeping with this same spirit of performance following knowledge, the information contained in this volume will help the reader discover that our mitzvot are not only to be observed but also to be enjoyed.

I wish to express my sincere appreciation to all those individuals who have given me of their time, knowledge and counsel in the writing of this book. First of all, I wish to thank my dear wife, Eve, my children, Marilyn and Simon Selber and Geraldine and Isaac Wiener, and my granddaughter, Rachel Ilana Selber, who is an inspiration to us all.

In addition, I want also to acknowledge my debt of deep gratitude to the following individuals who have contributed to the success of this volume:

To Rabbi Steven Riskin, of the Lincoln Square Synagogue of New York, for his general evaluation of the chapter on Kashrut, and to Rabbi Joseph Feinstein, Kashrut Administrator of Southern California, who also offered valuable pointers in the same area.

A special measure of thanks to Rabbi Tibor Stern, of Miami Beach, Florida, for his invaluable assistance and his authoritative suggestions with regard to the Kashrut chapter. I am grateful to Rabbi Yaakov Feitman for having read the manuscript and for his constructive suggestions.

I am further grateful to Rabbi Paysach Krone, of Kew Gardens, New York, for his constructive reading of the chapter on circumcision.

Thanks are due the Jacksonville Jewish Center and Congregation Beth Shalom of Jacksonville, Florida, for the use of their library facilities, and also to the libraries of Yeshiva University, the Jewish Theological Seminary of America, and the Los Angeles campus of the Hebrew Union College-Jewish Institute of Religion.

M.G.

Jacksonville, Florida
November, 1980
Kislev, 5741

Pidyon haBen coins, silver, issued by Bank of Israel in 1971.

BIRTH, CIRCUMCISION, AND
EARLY CHILDHOOD CEREMONIES
IN JEWISH LIFE

Perhaps the greatest thing that has ever happened to anybody is simply to have been born, and if we thank God for anything, it is for life itself and for bringing us into the world as Jews.

Every people has its own way of celebrating the birth of a new member, in the expectation that he will carry on the national traditions and ways of life.

We Jews celebrate the birth of a child with three specific ceremonies: *Brit Milah* (circumcision), naming, and *Pidyon ha-Ben* (redemption of the first-born). Only the second of these (naming) affects every Jewish child; the first (circumcision) applies only to a boy; and the third (*Pidyon ha-Ben*), only to most first-born males. An understanding of what goes into these ceremonies that take place in the early life of a Jew will prepare you for what lies ahead in later life.

BIRTH

A child is born Jewish only if he or she is born of a mother who either has been born Jewish, or has been converted to Judaism according to rabbinic law.

Even though they are not halakhically necessary, special prayers are often voluntarily offered during labor for the safety of both mother and child. During the Middle Ages it was often the custom to stay up all night before the birth of a child and before the circumcision, on a special vigil called *Wachnacht*, or "Watch Night," thus hoping to protect the child from being snatched away by evil spirits.

According to Jewish teaching, a child is born pure and untouched by sin. It is then up to him to continue as blameless throughout life.

CIRCUMCISION

Why Do We Have Circumcision?

Brit Milah, or the "Covenant of Circumcision," refers to the agreement God made with Abraham and his descendants for all generations, as an outward sign of which Abraham performed the ceremony of circumcision, first upon himself and then upon his sons and male servants.

Once before in human history had a sign been necessary to seal an agreement between God and man. After the Great Flood (Genesis 9:8-17), God had made a covenant with Noah promising that never again would there be a deluge that would destroy the whole world, and, as a constant reminder of this pledge, the rainbow was put in the sky. In the same way, as a continual reminder of God's promise to Abraham that He would make his descendants into a great nation, we have been given the sign of circumcision. This is a minor operation, originally prescribed by God to Abraham (Genesis 17:10), and is required to be performed on every male child when he is eight days old.

In the beginning of the chapter dealing with circumcision, God declared to Abraham, "I am God Almighty; walk before Me, and be wholehearted" (Genesis 17:1). Our rabbis teach us that circumcision is the way in which the Jew expresses his "wholehearted" faith in God.

It was precisely during those periods when circumcision was prohibited by the ruling powers that it took on new symbolic value and became a rallying point for Jewish self-affirmation, as in the Maccabean stand against the Syrians and in the Bar Kochba revolt against the Romans in 130 C.E. Even today circumcision is still under attack in the Soviet Union, where Jews cannot practice it without being persecuted and suffering untold hardship and disgrace.

The reason why Syria and Rome prohibited this simple ceremony on pain of death was that they understood its symbolic value, just as do the Soviets when they attack the practice of circumcision more severely than any other single Jewish practice. This, too, was what prompted many mothers to give up their own and their children's lives for their religion. Today, fortunately for us in this country, we can carry out the *mitzvah* of circumcision, as we can the whole of our religion, without such self-sacrifice being necessary.

The practice of circumcision has also been proved to be a good preventative of many diseases affecting the sex organs, and this is the reason why even many non-Jews choose to be circumcised. Of course, the Jew practices circumcision not for health reasons, but because, as has been stated above, he has been so commanded by God, and, as with all the other *mitzvot*, he receives the advantages that go along with the observance, whether the advantages are known or unknown to him. One of the special advantages here is that of health.

In fact, so strongly is this commandment ingrained in the lives of the Jewish people that many Jews who are not at all observant in other aspects still practice circumcision, and often this rite becomes their last remaining tie to Judaism.

If, on the other hand, a Jew has not been circumcised, he still remains a Jew, but a Jew by birth only, and not a wholehearted Jew. He has done nothing to demonstrate his link with his people, nor has he shown any proof that he has accepted the teachings of Judaism as his own.

At the age of eight days the young lad enters the Covenant by being circumcised. This ceremony makes him eligible to become a "wholehearted Jew." However, it will then be up to him to prove through his conduct as a Jew that he has actually earned this time-honored privilege.

During Biblical times no Jew was allowed to offer the Paschal Lamb sacrifice for Passover unless he had been circumcised (Exodus, 12:48). Our Sages tell us that the *mitzvah* of circumcision is equal to all the other commandments of our Torah, because it furnishes the evidence of our commitment to all the rest.

The "Shalom Zakhor" Ceremony

On the Friday night before the circumcision it is also customary to observe the "Shalom Zakhor" celebration. This familiar expression, *Shalom Zakhor*, means "peace unto the male child," which is based on the traditional belief, according to our sages, that "if a boy is born, peace comes into the world."

For this event relatives and friends gather at the home of the child's parents in order to wish them well. Following the recitation of the *Shema* prayer and certain other verses from the Bible, along with additional prayers for the welfare of the mother and her newborn son, the guests are served food, drinks, etc. Everyone present, of course, wishes the family the best for the *Brit* and for a happy and healthy life thereafter for the infant.

Circumcision as a Happy Occasion

A *Brit Milah* today is celebrated as a happy occasion, instead of being one of fear of those who would persecute the Jews for observing circumcision, as was often the case in times past. For this reason do we express our thanks and joy during this ceremony.

Since the eighth day was the time specified by God to Abraham (Genesis 17:12), *Brit Milah* must be performed exactly on the eighth day after birth, even if it should fall on a Sabbath, a festival, or Yom Kippur. The ceremony may be delayed only on grounds of the child's health.

By waiting until the eighth day, the child goes through a full week of good health. What is more, the clotting factor is much improved by that time.

The ceremony is usually performed during the morning, as a reminder of the fact that Abraham got up early in the morning in order to obey God's commandment.

The Mohel

During Biblical times circumcision would ordinarily be performed by the father of the child, although there is one case where even a mother undertook this operation (Exodus 4:24-26). Also, during the Maccabean period, when circumcision was prohibited on penalty of death, Jewish mothers would often risk their lives for this *mitzvah* (II Maccabees 6:10). Today, however, this operation is usually performed by a man who is specially trained for the task — a *mohel.*

The *mohel* must not only be an expert in this surgery; he must, at the same time, be learned in Torah, as well as being an observant Jew. It is a complete violation of Jewish law, although it is today a common practice, for a surgeon who is not a *mohel* to perform the circumcision, while a rabbi stands by and recites the blessings.

This is the case because it is not the rabbi's blessings that give the circumcision the stamp of holiness, but the operation of the *mohel.* A doctor can carry out a good surgical operation, but only a qualified *mohel* can perform it according to Jewish law.*

Besides the *mohel*, others who participate in the ceremony include:

1) The *sandek*, the one who holds the child during the *Brit.*

2) The *qwatter* (godfather) and the *qwatterin* (godmother) who hand the child to the *sandek.*

At every *Brit Milah* ceremony there is also a special chair set aside for Elijah the Prophet — the child's true guardian, according to tradition — whose spirit, it is believed, is capable of wishing good health for the child and a quick healing of the wound of circumcision.

It is desirable, but not necessary, to have a *minyan* present at the circumcision. The ceremony proceeds in the following order:

1) The mother hands over the child (who usually rests on a special pillow) to the godmother, who then hands it to the godfather.

*For further details regarding the circumcision operation, see *Encyclopedia Judaica*, Vol. V: 571-572; *Universal Jewish Encyclopedia*, III:214; or, *Jewish Encyclopedia*, IV: 99-102.

Embroidered decoration for circumcision ritual, gold thread on velvet, Germany, 1884.

2) The *qwatter* hands it to the father.

3) The *qwatter* or father places the child on the Chair of Elijah, and then the father places him on the *sandek's* lap, where the operation takes place.

4) The operation is performed by the *mohel.*

5) The father then recites a blessing expressing his thankfulness that his son has now been entered into the Covenant of Abraham.

6) The child is named.

7) Then follows the reception, usually consisting of refreshments and other forms of rejoicing.

During the reception everyone present expresses the wish that the child may grow up to qualify for the "study of Torah, marriage, and good deeds." The ceremony of circumcision thus gives us another opportunity to enjoy our Judaism and to take pride in our Jewish heritage.*

NAMING THE CHILD

A male child is named immediately after the circumcision operation, to remind us of how God changed Abram's name to Abraham following the latter's circumcision. Therefore, as a result of this double ceremony — the circumcision and naming — the child establishes his identity as a Jew in the following two ways:

*For further details of the ceremony, see *Encyclopedia Judaica,* V: 571-572; A.E. Kitov, *The Jew and His Home,* pp. 185-190; *Jewish Encyclopedia,* V: 95-96; *Universal Jewish Encyclopedia,* III: 214-215; H.L. Donin, *To Be A Jew,* pp. 273-276.

1) Physically, through the circumcision operation, and,

2) Spiritually, because as a result of his circumcision, he is expected to become as "wholehearted a Jew" as was his ancestor Abraham.

A girl receives her name in the synagogue on the first Sabbath (or on the Monday or Thursday) after her birth, when her father is called to the Torah. This event is often followed by a *Kiddush* after the services.

A child is usually named after a departed relative, so as to perpetuate the memory of that relative. Sephardic Jews, however, often name their children after living relatives.

The child's Hebrew name is expressed in the following form: "_____, the son of (the father's Hebrew name)" or for a girl, "_____, the daughter of (the father's Hebrew name)." If the child's father is a Kohen or a Levi, that title is also added. For example, "Moshe *ben* David, Halevi," or, for a girl, "Sarah *bat* David, Hakohen."

Normally, the child is given a Biblical, Israeli, or Yiddish name. However, if the Hebrew name given you at birth is to have any meaning, you must use it and have your parents, relatives, and friends call you by that name. This is another way of showing your pride in your Jewishness. But if you never use your Hebrew name, then you do not show respect for the person after whom you were called, because his or her memory is not perpetuated.

Your Hebrew and your English names may not always correspond. So, although the Hebrew name Moshe, for example, should become Moses, for reasons of personal preference a person might choose to be called Martin or some other popular English name. You must remember, however, that your Hebrew name will have no value for you unless it is used.*

PIDYON HA-BEN
(REDEMPTION OF THE FIRST-BORN)

Why Do We Observe Pidyon ha-Ben?

Pidyon ha-Ben is the Hebrew for the "redemption (or ransom) of the (first-born) son." Basically, we Jews believe that everything we own belongs to God. We remember this by giving back to Him a small portion of what we possess. That is why we give back to God the first-born of every animal and every human being (Numbers 18:15-16).

Before the sin of the Golden Calf, the first-born of Israel were to be the ones to perform the service in the future Sanctuary. However, when the entire tribe of Levi abstained from participation in that sin, they were granted the privilege of doing the service in the *Mishkan* — the Sanctuary which travelled with Israel, and later in the Holy Temple.

*For lists of Hebrew and English names, see A. J. Kolatch, *The Name Dictionary*, or N. Gottlieb, *A Jewish Child Is Born*.

הברת
בעלי בריה אברהם

Elijah's chair, Mantua, 18th century.

Since, initially, every first-born son does belong to God, it is the duty of every father to "buy him back" so that his child will not be required to take part in the divine service. Even if the circumcision has not yet been performed, we observe this ceremony on exactly the 31st day after birth, except if that day falls on a Sabbath or a festival.

A *Pidyon ha-Ben* occurs on the 31st day because, not counting the day on which the child was born, a full month must elapse before the ceremony is allowed to be performed.

During the ceremony, according to the Biblical command, the father gives the Kohen five silver pieces, the "ransom" for his son (Numbers 18:15-16).

How Is a Pidyon ha-Ben Ceremony Performed?

Every Jewish first-born, provided that it is a boy — who is not the product of a Cesarean birth — must have a *Pidyon ha-Ben*, unless the child's father or mother's father is a Kohen or a Levite.*

The ceremony, which is usually held at home, is a happy occasion, taking place in the presence of relatives and friends. While the father holds his son before the Kohen, the following conversation is spoken:

Father: My wife has borne me this first-born son.

Kohen: Which do you prefer, to give your son to me or to redeem him for 5 silver coins as the Torah commands?

Father: To redeem him and here is the money as commanded by the Torah.

A few blessings are then recited, and the father gives the five pieces of silver to the Kohen. Following the special blessings made by the Kohen, the ceremony ends with his recitation of the benediction over the wine. Refreshments usually conclude this joyous occasion.

Although the child has been formally redeemed, his duty as a first-born son does not end there. As soon as he is old enough, he must fast every *Erev Pesah*, the day when all the first-born of the Egyptians were killed, and those of the Israelites were saved. He need not fast, however, if he attends a *Siyyum ha-Torah*, which is a special occasion that marks the completion of the study of a Talmud tractate. Whenever Jews finish the study of a sacred book, especially a Talmud tractate, they hold a small celebration. Therefore, in order to relieve the first-born sons of their duty to fast, some section of the Talmud is completed on *Erev Pesah*, and the fast is turned into a celebration.

What Value Is There in a Pidyon ha-Ben?

Just as it is true for so many other commandments, the *Pidyon ha-Ben* ceremony, because it ties us that much closer to the laws and traditions of our Torah, enables us to respect our Torah that much more and to deepen our loyalty to Jewish tradition.

*For other conditions as to who is, or is not, required to have a *Pidyon ha-Ben*, see H.H. Donin, *To Be A Jew*, p. 277; or, A.E. Kitov, *The Jew and His Home*, pp. 196-197.

16

A tray for redemption ceremony, Poland, 19th century.

The *Pidyon ha-Ben* ceremony reminds us that we must give to God only the best of all that we earn or own, and not just what is left over. Two Bible stories will illustrate this point. The first is that of the kind of offerings Cain and Abel made to God (Genesis 4:3-16), and the second is that of Abraham showing his willingness to offer up his beloved son, Isaac, as a sacrifice (Genesis 22:1-19). In both these cases, what was offered and accepted by God was nothing but the best.

Although you may have earned many fine things through your own efforts, you must remember that it is only with God's help that you have come to have them. It is He who gives you life, health, and everything else. Therefore, you must be ready to give up all these wonderful things, should such a sacrifice be demanded of you. Throughout our long history many Jews were often called upon to sacrifice even their lives for Judaism. You, fortunately, are being asked to give up much less than that.

These are some of the things you should think about the next time you witness a *Pidyon ha-Ben* ceremony.

*Bronze coin issued by Bank of Israel in 1964
on the occasion of the 3rd International Bible
Contest.*

JEWISH EDUCATION

Did you know that the Jewish people are sometimes called *Am ha-Sefer*, "The People of the Book"?

Throughout Jewish history, Jews have placed a high value on study and scholarship. Moses Maimonides, the famous philosopher, Talmudist, and physician (1135-1204), wrote that every Jew must keep studying as long as he lives. Why have Jews always loved learning so much? What must Jews study in order to understand the laws, customs, traditions, and values of Judaism? How do we go about acquiring this timeless knowledge?

THE JEWISH LOVE OF LEARNING

In most of the ancient civilizations, education was regarded as the privilege of the select few — royalty, priests, and the wealthy upper classes. The common people usually remained ignorant. In fact, the ruling classes often felt that it was better for the masses not to know too much so that they would not question the orders given them by the authorities. Futhermore, most of the plain folk felt no desire for any knowledge beyond those basic skills that they needed for their daily

Congregation B'nai Torah
700 Mt Vernon Hwy NE
Atlanta GA 30328

living: hunting, fishing, farming sheep and cattle raising, homebuilding, woodcarving, and clothesmaking. Even in our own day it is often thought sufficient for a man or woman to know merely how to make a living. Studies beyond the "3 R's" and the basic vocational skills are looked on as "extras." Most people still consider their education to be complete once they have left their school days behind.

It was never so with the Jewish people. Naturally, our sages insisted that every Jew should be taught some trade or occupation that would enable him to earn a livelihood. As a matter of fact, our rabbis went so far as to state that a father who did not teach his son a useful occupation was teaching him to be a thief (for if he would not be able to earn a living, he would eventually be forced to steal in order not to starve). Nor did our scholars, even in ancient times, neglect the skills of the body. According to the Talmud (*Kiddushin* 29a), it is the duty of a father even to teach his son how to swim. But the education of the Jewish child was not considered as having ended with his training in the things he had to know in order to make a living or to develop his body, nor did Judaism ever regard the end of formal schooling as the end of the obligation to study. Every day, for thousands of years, the observant Jew has recited in the *Shema* prayer the passage from the Five Books of Moses (Deuteronomy 6:4-9) that defines the all-important position Judaism assigns to study:

> And these words which I command you this day shall be upon your heart. You shall teach them diligently to your children, and you shall speak of them when you are sitting in your house, when you walk upon your way, when you lie down and when you rise up. You shall bind them as a sign upon your hand, and they shall be for frontlets between your eyes. You shall inscribe them upon the doorposts of your house and upon your gates.

From the age of three on, regardless of whether he was rich or poor, of noble descent or of humble origins, gifted with a brilliant mind or equipped with only modest intelligence, every Jew was expected to devote a significant part of his time, not only while he was of school age but also throughout his life, to the study of Torah.

Torah is the Hebrew term for "teaching" or "guidance." Specifically, the term applies to the Five Books of Moses (Pentateuch), in which are laid down the basic moral, social, civil, and religious laws that govern the relationship of a Jew to God and to his fellowman. In a broader sense, however, Torah includes all of Judaism's religious-ethical literature. This encompasses not only the "Written Law" of the Bible but also the "Oral Law," the immense body of rabbinic law (the Talmud) that was given together with the "Written Law" at Mount Sinai, that expands upon the Biblical laws, and that was transmitted by word of mouth over the centuries before it was finally set down in writing. In addition, Torah comprises all the many rabbinical codes and commentaries on Biblical and Talmudic law that have been written by early sages and later rabbinic authorities from the Middle Ages down to our own day.

"Studying the Talmud," oil by Isidor Kaufman, Austria (1853-1921).

This entire vast body of knowledge is referred to as Torah because its teachings are intended to serve us as a "guide" in our actions from the time we rise each morning until we retire for the night, every day of our lives, from the age when we first become aware of ourselves as individuals, and for our entire lifetime. The Torah explains our duties to our fellowman and to God and teaches us how to live happily and properly. Nevertheless, these are but a few of the things we learn and gain from the study of Torah.

Our grandfathers used to say that *Toyre iz de beste s'khoyra* (Torah is the best merchandise of all). It is not just a "subject" with no practical value, to be studied as one might study philosophy or literature or ancient history, an extra "specialty" to enrich our knowledge and culture but without relevance to our daily life. Not at all. Torah teaches us all the things we need to know in order to be able to follow our Jewish way of life.

But because of our great reverence and love for the Torah, we also study it for its own sake, for the pure pleasure we gain from its study and simply because to study is one of the primary commandments.

Throughout our history, even those who were not able, or chose not, to become great scholars were not excused from the lifelong obligation to study. It was always taken as a matter of course that every Jew had to have an elementary knowledge of the Five Books of Moses and of the laws they contain. To this end, in ancient Palestine portions of the Five Books of Moses were read aloud to the public on various stated occasions — on Sabbaths, on holidays, and also, in the larger towns of Palestine, on Mondays and Thursdays, the market days on which Jewish farmers would flock to towns and cities to sell their produce. After the destruction of the Second Temple (70 C.E.), the "reading from the Torah" gradually gained a central place in the synagogue services on Sabbaths, festivals, and Mondays and Thursdays. Even before the fall of the Second Jewish Commonwealth, Jews would meet in small groups throughout Palestine to recite prayers and to be instructed in Biblical law. From that time on — over two thousand years ago — and continuing to our own present day, Jews have been expected, at the very least, to be able to follow the readings from the Torah and to be familiar with the prayers, some of which present the laws and teachings of Judaism in a simple, easy-to-understand manner. Also, long before "adult education" became a household term in modern life, Jews were expected to attend *shiurim*, lectures by individuals well-versed in Jewish law, as often as possible. This practice began in ancient Palestine and has continued in our synagogues the world over.

In this manner, throughout the ages, the teachers and spiritual leaders of the Jewish people sought to make sure that even those with only a limited capacity for study would acquire the fundamentals of Torah, so that everyone would observe the laws of Judaism not only as a matter of unquestioned routine but with a true understanding of their significance as well.

In view of all the foregoing, it should not come as a surprise to learn that the Jews were among the first (if not actually *the* first) people to establish schools for all children and to make school attendance compulsory. In the United States, compulsory education became the law of the land only about one hundred and fifty years ago; among the Jewish people, it had become the rule two thousand years before in ancient Palestine. To stress the importance of education to the Jews even at that early date, our rabbis relate that King Hezekiah (who reigned over the southern kingdom of Judah nearly twenty-seven hundred years ago) had planted a sword by the door of every schoolhouse proclaiming that "he who will not study the Torah will be pierced with (this) sword." We are further told that all of Palestine, from Dan to Beersheba, was searched, but that no ignoramus was found and that there was no man or woman, boy or girl, who was not thoroughly versed in the laws of purity and impurity, which are among the most difficult and complex laws of Judaism (Talmud, Sanhedrin 94b).

A fully observant Jew studies Torah not only because he is commanded to do so or because he expects to receive honors for it, but because he cannot conceive of life without it. We need only to recall the story of Hillel, the president of the Great Sanhedrin, who lived about two thousand years ago and whose zeal for study nearly cost him his life. One wintry day, when the then young student did not have the money for the admission fee to the house of study, he stretched himself out on the skylight of the school so that he might hear the lecture delivered inside. He was so engrossed in the lecture that he did not even feel the snow fall on him, and he would probably have frozen to death had not someone inside noticed a shadow blocking the light, gone out to investigate, and found Hillel there.

Rabbi Akiba ben Joseph (about 50-132 C.E.), we are told, started out in life as an ignorant shepherd, but after his marriage he left his wife (and children) to spend over twenty years in the uninterrupted study of Torah. He is remembered today as the greatest scholar of Jewish law during the period immediately following the destruction of the Second Temple. Incidentally, the story has it that Rabbi Akiba set out on his career of study upon the insistence of his wife.

Driven by this passionate love for Torah, Jews the world over have often done without the necessities of life in order to study the Law. It was considered a good deed to provide food for poor students of Torah and to support the institutions where Torah was taught. Householders who themselves did not have an opportunity to study very much made sacrifices to enable their sons to do so, or their daughters to marry young men who would spend full time at study for the first few years following their marriage.

Among some very observant Jews, it is still considered a matter of personal pride and prestige for a father to support a son-in-law who studies at a Talmudic academy (Yeshiva) and who gives promise of becoming a scholar in the Law. There are young men today who attend college only in the evenings in order to spend their days at Torah study; others take off a year or more for full-time Yeshiva study before continuing their secular training at a university, or before entering a graduate school. Other young men and women attend universities where they may take up secular studies and "learn Torah" under the same roof.

Jews have come to cherish the study of Torah even more because it has helped sustain the Jewish people through centuries of homelessness and persecution. In the ghettos, the Jew would turn to Torah study for comfort; the wisdom of the Torah reminded him of the

Illustration from the Prague edition of the Pentateuch, 1530.

Bronze coin issued by Bank of Israel in 1973.

unique role of his people in the history of human civilization as the "People of the Book" and kept alive within him a sense of pride in his age-old heritage. Survivors of the Nazi Holocaust have told soul-stirring tales of "underground" Talmud classes in ghettos and even in the concentration camps. Torah study has also taken its place in the rebirth of the Jewish people in the modern State of Israel; it is part of the regular training program of the Israeli defense forces. Those who saw on their television screens the footage of the 1973 Yom Kippur War will never forget the picture of the Israeli soldiers going into Egyptian captivity, led by a soldier proudly bearing a Scroll of the Law in his arms. When the tide of the war turned and Israeli troops crossed the Suez Canal into Egyptian territory, young scholars in uniform organized Torah classes for the fighting men there.

Thus, for thousands of years, in joy and in sorrow, in exile and in triumph, Torah study has held a central position in Jewish religious and national life. Today, whether they use the traditional term "Torah learning" or the more modern "Jewish education," all Jews concerned with the survival of Judaism agree on the essential role which Jewish learning plays in keeping alive the individual's sense of identity as a member of the Jewish people.

WHAT DOES "JEWISH EDUCATION" INCLUDE TODAY?

What should Jews study in order to gain a better understanding of their Jewish heritage and their own role in Jewish life today? Modern "Jewish education" includes both purely religious studies and studies that while not strictly part of religious training, will serve to strengthen the student's feeling of Jewish identity.

Religious Studies

I.   The Bible —Written Law
     The Bible is divided into three main parts: *Torah* (The Five Books of Moses), *Neviim* (Prophets), and *Ketubim* (Holy Writings).

Hitul for Sefer Torah, cloth, Denmark, 1801.

A. *Torah* (Pentateuch)

The Five Books of Moses open with the story of the creation of the world, and then proceed to relate the beginnings of the Jewish people (the lives of the Patriarchs: Abraham, Isaac, and Jacob) and the story of the exodus from Egypt. They go on to describe the wanderings of the Children of Israel through the wilderness on their way to the Promised Land and set forth the Ten Commandments and the religious, civil, and ethical laws, which were revealed to Moses on Mount Sinai. The Pentateuch concludes with the death of Moses within sight of the Promised Land. Because it contains the basic laws of Judaism, the Pentateuch is often referred to as the "constitution" of the Jewish people, inasmuch as all explanatory laws must agree with those of the Torah.

B. *Neviim* (Prophets)

1. Early Prophets

The books of Joshua, Judges, Samuel I and II, and Kings I and II. These books are primarily historical in nature, presenting the story of the Jewish people from the time they first entered the Promised Land until the destruction of the First Temple in the year 586 B.C.E.

2. Later Prophets

The fifteen books that come under this heading record the teachings of the Prophets, who conveyed to the Jewish people the message of God. The Prophets served as teachers and guides, stressing the importance of justice and morality; only through a life based on righteous and ethical conduct could the Jewish people become the "holy nation" it was meant to be. The works of the Later Prophets include the three Major Prophets — Isaiah, Jeremiah, and Ezekiel — and the twelve Minor Prophets — Hosea, Joel, Amos,

Torah crown, 18th century.

Obadiah, Jonah, Micah, Nahum, Habakkuk, Zephaniah, Haggai, Zechariah, and Malachi. (The adjectives "major" and "minor" in this instance are not meant to class the prophets in terms of their importance. The Minor Prophets are so called merely because the books recording their messages are shorter than those containing the teachings of Isaiah, Jeremiah, and Ezekiel.)

C. *Ketubim* (Holy Writings)

These thirteen books include works of history, poetry, and wisdom, and all share a concern with God and His commandments. They include the Books of Psalms, Proverbs, Job (which seeks to answer the question why righteous people sometimes suffer), the Five Scrolls (Ruth, Esther, Lamentations, Ecclesiastes, and Song of Songs), Daniel, Ezra, Nehemiah, and Chronicles I and II.

II. The Talmud — Oral Law

This book of laws, which explains the Written Law, is known as the *Talmud*, or Oral Law. As distinct from the Written Law, the laws and rabbinical statements contained in the Talmud were passed down by word of mouth for generations before being set down in writing. The Talmud consists of the six books, or "orders," of the Mishnah, and the sixty-three tractates of the Gemara, which explain the Mishnah. The six orders of the

Mishnah are: (1) *Zera'im* ("seeds"), dealing with the laws pertaining to agriculture and prayers; (2) *Mo'ed* ("seasons"), dealing with the observance of Sabbaths and festivals; (3) *Nashim* ("women"), dealing with marriage, divorce, and vows; (4) *Nezikin* ("damages"), dealing with civil and criminal law; (5) *Kodashim* ("holy things"), dealing with ritual slaughter, sacred objects, and the sacrificial ritual; (6) *Taharot* ("purities"), dealing with the laws of ritual purity.

The Talmud is not an easy subject; its study requires competent instruction and guidance, but it can be mastered with continuous study. Long years spent in Talmudic learning not only produce an expert knowledge of Jewish law but also tend to sharpen the mind. It has often been claimed that the special aptitude among Jews for sciences and other studies requiring keen logic comes from an age-old background of mental exercise through the study of Talmud.

III.   Rabbinic Codes

Almost all the laws of the Talmud have been summarized in a code of laws, the *Shulḥan Arukh* (literally, "prepared table"), compiled by Rabbi Joseph Karo, a noted scholar who lived during the sixteenth century. The work consists of four sections: (1) *Oraḥ Ḥayyim* — the laws pertaining to prayer, public worship, and the observance of the Sabbath and festivals; (2) *Yoreh Deah* — laws pertaining to mourning, circumcision, prohibition of idol worship, and *Kashrut*; (3) *Eben Ha-Ezer* — laws of marriage and divorce; (4) *Hoshen Mishpat* — civil and criminal laws. As explanations of all of the above listed holy books, countless others have been written giving interpretations of older as well as more recent scholars.

IV.   The Midrash (literally, "inquiry")

This is a class of books that further interpret the Torah through searching for deeper and hidden meanings in its words by using fanciful stories, tales, wise sayings, and other methods. Some of this material was delivered as sermons by the rabbis, who would thus try to explain the meaning of the Torah in a very simple manner to the common people during synagogue services on Sabbaths and festivals.

Bronze coin issued by Bank of Israel in 1964 on the occasion of the 3rd International Bible Contest.

The oldest Hebrew Biblical manuscript in the Jewish National and University Library, Jerusalem.

V. Responsa

These consist of questions on matters of religious observance, posed to great rabbinic authorites on Jewish law, and the rulings handed down in reply by these authorities. The Responsa span a period of over a thousand years; thus far, about the same number of volumes containing more than half a million "questions and answers" have appeared in print. Many of them make fascinating reading because they reflect the life and the problems of Jewish communities throughout the world over the centuries. More recent Responsa dealing with the application of rabbinic law to modern-day issues such as service in the army, medical ethics, etc., are of particular interest.

VI. General Religious Studies

A. *Siddur* (Jewish Prayer Book)

A basic Jewish education should include not only learning to read and recite the daily, Sabbath, and holiday prayers, but also a knowledge of the general order and arrangement of these prayers.

In addition, many English commentaries published by rabbis and scholars can be found in the *Siddur*. These help us to gain a deeper understanding of the prayers.

The *Siddur* should become the close companion of every Jew.

B. Customs and Ceremonies

The joys of observing the Sabbaths, the holidays, and other Jewish ceremonies (Bar Mitzvahs, weddings, etc.) are much enhanced by learning the background of these observances.

In the process of learning about the customs and ceremonies, you also come into contact with other Jewish subjects. So, for example, in order to properly understand the observance of Passover, you have to use the Bible, the *Haggadah*, the prayerbook, and portions of the Talmud and Jewish history, all of which you thus get to know that much better.

"Secular" Jewish Studies

While these studies are not strictly part of religious training, they are important for our understanding of the Jewish people, past and present, and are an additional help to us in identifying with our past and with our fellow Jews the world over.

I. The Hebrew Language

To know Hebrew is to be able to study the Bible, much of the Talmud, the prayer book, and all of the other holy books listed above in their original form. A translation, no matter how accurate, cannot be relied upon to transmit the limitless wisdom of our heritage.

A knowledge of Hebrew can also take you through our literature, so rich in short stories, novels, poems, and history.

The Hebrew language is still another link that binds us to our past — to our fellow Jews who have shared the same language for

Simḥat Torah scene in Jerusalem by Chaim Gross.

thousands of years. This link can be felt most deeply by every Jew who visits or lives in the State of Israel, where Hebrew is the official language — the only one shared by Jews from all over the world.

II. Yiddish

Lately, there has been an increasing interest in the study of the Yiddish language and Yiddish literature. Young people, particularly on the college campuses, have turned to Yiddish to help them gain a more complete picture of Jewish life in the *shtetls* of Eastern Europe and of early Jewish immigrant life in the United States. Although many important works of Yiddish literature have been translated into English and other languages, no translation can entirely recapture the flavor and spirit of the original.

III. Jewish History

Of all the peoples on earth, the Jews, backed by four thousand years of history, have contributed more to world civilization than has any other people known to mankind. Jews have played an important part in the history of almost every leading nation in the world.

A knowledge of our own history, in addition to making us proud to be Jews, is an essential aid to the understanding of the issues and problems facing the Jewish people today. It also enables us to answer questions that non-Jewish people ask about Judaism and to clear up misunderstandings that sometimes give rise to anti-Jewish prejudices.

Discussions of current events affecting Judaism and Jewish communities bring our history up-to-date and keep us in constant touch with the interests and concerns of our fellow Jews in other cities and countries all over the world.

IV. Israel

A knowledge of the land of Israel goes hand in hand with the study of the Bible, the Talmud, history, and many other Jewish subjects. This tiny country has been so closely tied to Jewish life that it cannot be separated from anything that is Jewish. In fact, as our rabbis tell us, Israel, the Torah, and the Jewish people are all one single, inseparable unity. Since Israel is the Jewish homeland, its history, geography, culture, and so much more should be familiar to every Jew.

This knowledge helps us to see how Israel has influenced the course of world history, and enables us to better appreciate Israel's position in the world today.

HOW TO ACQUIRE JEWISH KNOWLEDGE

Early Beginnings

Legend has it that the mother of Rabbi Joshua ben Ḥananiah, a great rabbinic scholar who lived nearly two thousand years ago, would bring her son to the "house of study" when he was still an infant in his cradle. She did this in the hope that the baby's ears would gradually become accustomed to the sounds of the voices of teachers and students discussing the wisdom of the Torah — so that the Torah would thus become as natural to him as his mother's milk.

In much the same manner, the Jewish child growing up in a home where Jewish traditions are observed will gain his earliest knowledge of Judaism long before he enters a Jewish school, where such things are formally taught. He will see his mother light the Sabbath candles, he will see and hear his father reciting the prayers, and before long he will be taught to recite some short prayers and blessings himself, such as the *Modeh Ani* (the short morning prayer giving thanks to God for another day about to begin), the *Shema Yisrael* (recited in the morning and again before going to bed), blessings before and after eating, and blessings to be said on certain occasions, such as the putting on of new clothes. As the child grows older, he will be taken to the synagogue; the earlier he begins to go to the synagogue, the more likely he will soon feel at home there. Young children particularly enjoy those services in which they themselves can take an active part: the Friday night *Kiddush*, when they may go up to the cantor and perhaps receive a little of the sweet *Kiddush* wine; *Purim*, when they may use *graggers* and other noisemakers to drown out the name of the wicked Haman, who wanted to destroy the Jewish people; and *Simhat Torah*, when they receive apples, candy, and gaily colored flags, and may march and dance in the joyous procession with the Scrolls of the Law.

By the time a child is four or five years old, he or she may be enrolled in a nursery school or kindergarten run by a synagogue or by a Jewish Day School. There the boys and girls are taught Hebrew songs and games, and there are "parties" with games and refreshments to help them learn how to observe the Sabbath and the holidays.

Elementary Jewish Education

Following nursery or kindergarten, the Jewish child's formal education begins. If he goes to public school, he may attend a Hebrew school or *Talmud Torah* on weekday afternoons and Sunday mornings. These schools may be part of the synagogue he attends, or they may be supported by the Jewish community as a whole. There, the child learns how to read, write, and speak Hebrew, and how to read the prayer book. He also studies Jewish history, customs, and ceremonies. Later on, he begins to study the Five Books of Moses. When boys reach the age of twelve, they receive the special training they need to prepare them for their *Bar Mitzvah* (which is discussed in another chapter).

Some children, instead of attending public school during the morning and early afternoon, and Hebrew school only in the late afternoons and on Sundays, go to a Hebrew Day School, where public-school subjects are taught along with Jewish studies. Children attending such a school (known as *Yeshiva Katana*, or "little Yeshiva") have a chance to get a more thorough Jewish education and to advance with greater speed to Bible and Talmud, than children who study

Hebrew only a few hours each week, and then only in the late afternoon, when they are already tired from their schoolday. At some Day Schools Jewish subjects are taught during the morning hours and public-school studies during the early afternoon; in others a period of "Hebrew" is followed by one of "English," and so on throughout the day. Another advantage of the Day School is that the everyday customs of Judaism may be observed there in a much more natural manner than at a public school. For instance, at lunchtime the children at a Day School will find it quite natural to recite the proper prayers before and after meals. And when the Jewish holidays arrive, the day-school child does not have the problem of missing any of his "English" studies, as he would in a public school, which is open on the Jewish holidays.

Secondary Jewish Education

From the *Talmud Torah*, a boy or girl may go on to a Hebrew high school, which, like the *Talmud Torah*, meets on weekday afternoons and on Sundays. There, the student continues his studies in Bible, Jewish history, and laws and customs on a higher level. He will also take such subjects as Jewish philosophy and Hebrew literature. In a Day School, the student graduates from elementary to high school in both "Hebrew" and "English" subjects. The subjects studied include *Tanakh* (Torah, *Neviim* and *Ketubim*), *dinim* (the everyday laws and customs of Judaism), history, and literature, but now the emphasis is placed, especially for the boys, on the study of the Talmud.

However, today even many public schools (especially in the larger cities) offer Hebrew as a foreign language, and it is generally accepted for college entrance credit, just as is any other foreign language, such as French, Spanish, etc.

After a young person is graduated from high school, there are many alternatives open to him or her for advanced Jewish studies.

A young man wishing to devote his full time to studying the Talmud may go to a Yeshiva in order to increase his Jewish knowledge and, perhaps, to become a rabbi.

Today, many young men and women are able to attend Jewish universities that offer both Jewish and secular courses; this option allows the student to acquire advanced Jewish learning as well as to take courses leading to a Bachelor's degree. A degree may also be earned in Jewish studies.

Or, one may enroll in a Hebrew college, either on a part-time or full-time basis, while working or attending a secular university.

An increasing number of secular universities throughout the United States have established departments of Jewish studies. In this situation students may take courses and will receive credit towards graduation just as they would in any of the other departments of the institution.

"Great Laws," the first code to give a detailed list of the 613 precepts which are included in the Torah.

Adult Education

By far the best time to begin a Jewish education is at a young age when one's mind is clear and fresh and when learning is easiest. The knowledge gained at that time remains with you the longest. But because it is never too late to begin studying about your heritage, and because Jewish education is a lifelong process that must never be regarded as complete, there are many opportunities for Jewish adults to continue — or even begin — their acquisition of Jewish knowledge.

Our rabbis tell us that every Jew must set aside a portion of each day for Torah study, which can be achieved either privately, on one's own, or in a class or group situation.

Synagogues sponsor *shiurim* (Talmudic lectures) for those who are familiar with the Talmud; they also arrange lecture courses on the Bible, laws and customs, Jewish history, Jewish literature, Jewish philosophy, prayers, and the Hebrew language. Similar courses are sponsored by Jewish community centers and other Jewish organizations. In this manner those who are working full time may continue their Jewish studies on an informal basis in the evenings or perhaps on Sunday mornings. Some of the courses are advanced, but many more are on an intermediate level, and there are also beginners' courses (including elementary Hebrew reading) for those who did not receive a Jewish education when they were young.

Still another way to continue your Jewish learning is by reading the many Jewish newspapers and magazines in which articles by some very learned scholars and other items of interest appear. Of course, a large number of books on a broad range of Jewish topics are published every year and are easily available.

WHAT VALUE IS THERE IN JEWISH LEARNING

The most important value of Jewish education is that it enables us to learn just what it is that God expects of us as Jews. The laws were given to us to live by, but we must know what they are in order to practice Judaism properly.

Throughout our history, Jewish education has helped to keep us alive as Jews. One of the reasons why we Jews have survived as a people and outlived so many other nations — most of which were so much stronger and more numerous than we — is that we have always been a learned people, and the study of Torah has always been very close to our hearts. Just as a father would teach his son, so did that son teach his son, and so on throughout the ages. The light of Torah never went out, but always shone brightly from one generation to another. Thus, for example, during the Middle Ages (or Dark Ages), while most other peoples were ignorant and unlearned, there was hardly a Jew who could not read and understand the Torah, as well as many other Jewish books.

So, as far as you are concerned, you are here as a Jew primarily because your father and all those before him studied their Judaism and passed that knowledge on to you. It is thus hoped that you will likewise pass that same torch of learning on to the generation after you and, in this way, do your share to keep its flame aglow for those who will follow in the future.

Furthermore, if you know Hebrew and can follow the prayers and the service, you will feel that much more at home in the synagogue, where you, as a Jew, *should* feel comfortable and natural. Knowing Hebrew and thus being able to pray as other Jews pray will give you the feeling that Hebrew is *your* language, that the prayers you are reciting are *your* prayers, and that the services are *your* services. Your sense of belonging will be complete.

As you pray in the synagogue, you will come to realize that you are in the company not only of those Jews in your own synagogue but also of all the other Jews all over the world who say these same prayers, at the same times, and in the same holy language — Hebrew. In this

"Studying the Talmud," woodcut by Joseph Budko.

way will you also feel yourself drawn that much closer to your people, and you will thereby soon discover how proud you are to be a Jew. Your Jewish knowledge will thus bring you an unparalleled sense of well-being that you will experience again and again.

We Jews have always valued learning so highly that the greatest shame a Jew could suffer would be to be called an *am ha-aretz*, an "ignoramus," while, on the other hand, the most highly respected person among us has always been called a *lamdan*, a man of learning. This is one reason why today, in the State of Israel, the illiteracy rate among our people is perhaps close to the lowest in the world.

No matter what his occupation and regardless of whether he is rich or poor, the Jew who is learned in the ways of Torah is worthy of the greatest respect. Thus, in the synagogue, any Jew who can recite the prayers correctly is permitted to lead the service as cantor. You have already been told about the great scholar, Hillel. He became the president of the Sanhedrin (the highest Jewish court) simply because he showed himself to be more learned than all the other scholars, despite his extreme poverty. For the same reason did many other great Jewish scholars become famous for their learning, even though they too had suffered from poverty and deprivation.

However, the Jew has gained from the study of Torah in still another way. As we have seen, the study of Torah, Talmud, and all other such subjects requires a great deal of thought and understanding, a keen memory, deep concentration, and analysis.

By having developed such mental habits, the Jew has been able to acquire much knowledge in addition to his Torah learning. It is therefore not surprising that among the world's greatest scholars, scientists, Nobel Prize winners, mathematicians, poets, and other professionals, you will always find quite a number of Jews.

Also, it is a known fact that even though at present we Jews account for no more than about 3% of the total population of the United States, our representation on the college campuses far exceeds that percentage. Over 80% of our college-age youth attend colleges and universities, while the national average is only approximately 30%. This is no doubt a result of the high esteem in which learning — both Jewish and secular — is held among our people.

It is likewise not surprising to find that students of Hebrew Day Schools (where Hebrew and general studies are taught in the same school) usually achieve the highest grades in statewide and other scholarship examinations.

But in the final analysis, it stands to reason that the more learned you are in Torah studies, the more likely you will be to lead a life of Torah living, inasmuch as your knowledge of Torah will help to shape your life.

Learning and observance go hand in hand for us Jews. As we learn, we become eager to experience the beauty of the Jewish way of life for ourselves, and this observance in turn leads us to seek still greater depths and heights of knowledge pertaining to our cherished heritage.

Finally, remember this: Torah knowledge is a rare treasure that no one can ever take away from you. It will be the best and most faithful friend you will ever have. All you have to do to get it is to want it and seek it — and it will be yours forever.

Bar Mitzvah coin, bronze, silver and gold, issued by the Bank of Israel in 1961 and 1971.

BAR MITZVAH

In today's world practically every Jew knows about the Bar Mitzvah ceremony. No doubt you also know that it takes place in the synagogue on Sabbath, followed by a party prepared by the parents.

That is not all there is to a Bar Mitzvah, however. First, let us try to find out what is involved in becoming Bar Mitzvah and where it leads to in later life. More than the actual ceremony itself, it is what comes before and after your Bar Mitzvah that counts.

The real question is: "What does becoming Bar Mitzvah actually mean?"

Every year you have a birthday. Some birthdays are more memorable than others, but, of all your birthdays, your 13th is the one you will most remember. Because, on reaching 13 years and a day, you become an adult Jew. (This extra day is added to make sure that you have reached a full 13 years.) Of course, it is obvious that, at age 13, you are not ready to take on the full responsibility of adult life, although it might have been different in the past. Still, since our rabbis have said that at that age a boy should be prepared to fulfill the *mitzvot* (commandments) of the Torah, that is the age marking Jewish maturity to this day.

Although you may not feel that you are fully mature, the Bar Mitzvah ceremony will serve as a reminder of what you are striving for: full responsibility for the observance of the commandments of our Torah.

In order to learn what you have to do so that you will lead a full Jewish life, you must first understand the responsibilities involved.

In your Hebrew studies you will have to become familiar with some of the *mitzvot*. (In fact, the term Bar Mitzvah means "a son of the *mitzvot*.") It is only when you are 13 or over that you will be able to discriminate between what is permitted and what is forbidden in Jewish law.

During the Bar Mitzvah ceremony you are given an opportunity to demonstrate in public that you intend to make the Torah an integral part of your life based on its *mitzvot*.

In fact, this is perhaps one of the fundamental reasons for the synagogue ceremony. Otherwise, there would be no need for it. Just as you become an American citizen at birth without having to do anything about it, so, as a Jew, you automatically become Bar Mitzvah on reaching the age of 13 and a day. Whether you have a ceremony or not, you are entitled to all the rights and privileges, and you are responsible for fulfilling all of the obligations, of an adult Jew.

This ceremony, however, gives you an opportunity to make a public declaration of your intention not only to take on the *mitzvot*, but also to become an active member of the Jewish people. Also, as you chant the blessings and the Torah and *Haftorah* portions, you are demonstrating to the congregation your Hebrew skills.

Finally, when you reach the age of Bar Mitzvah, you are, in effect, standing on the threshold of a new life.

You now have an opportunity to think about what lies ahead for you as a Jew, what you are going to study, and how you can be of greater service to the Jewish people. It is probably only the Bar Mitzvah ceremony that has made you think of these things.

HOW DO YOU BECOME BAR MITZVAH?

Since this is such a unique occasion to which your parents and you have so eagerly been looking forward, and since you can perform this ceremony only once in your whole life, you should do your utmost to prepare yourself properly for it. In general, you ought to have a good grounding in Jewish studies by the time you reach the age of Bar Mitzvah — in such subjects as Hebrew, Jewish history, Bible, prayers, customs, and ceremonies. This kind of preparation already starts a few years prior to your Bar Mitzvah.

You should not study the subjects only in order to become Bar Mitzvah, since they will be of use to you throughout your entire life. In order to master the special skills required for your Bar Mitzvah ceremony, however, you must be able to take this kind of background knowledge for granted.

About six months or a year before your Bar Mitzvah, you will begin to study the following:

1) The blessings for the Torah and the *Haftorah*.
2) Your special *Haftorah* portion.
3) Your special Torah portion.
4) The use of *tallit* and *tefillin*, including some of the laws connected with these sacred objects; how to put them on correctly; and the prayers and blessings associated with them.
5) The synagogue prayers, especially those for the Sabbath.
6) The special accents, or *Trop* (notes), for the chanting of the Torah and *Haftorah*.

Tefillin cases (phylacteries), silver, engraved, Poland, 19th century.

Here is what is involved in each of these subjects:

1) The Torah and *Haftorah* blessings, recited before and after the Torah or *Haftorah* reading, are always the same every week.

2) The *Haftorah*, a portion taken from the books of the Prophets, is in some way always related to the weekly Torah portion. Thus, for example, when in the Torah we read about the building of the Tabernacle in the desert in the time of Moses, we then read in the *Haftorah* about the building of the Temple by King Solomon. Every *Haftorah* portion is chanted with a special melody called *Trop*.

Most of the remaining subjects listed above can best be explained by a brief description of the Sabbath morning service that takes place on the day of the Bar Mitzvah.

First, there is a regular Sabbath *Shaḥarit* (morning) service. If you are able to lead the service by serving as a cantor, you will probably be invited to do so. You might also be asked to chant the prayers that are recited as the Torah is removed from, and later returned to, the Ark. Seven or more adult men (aged 13 or over) are called to the Torah to recite the blessings before and after each of the seven portions of the Torah reading.

If you are not actually going to read a *Haftorah*, you may be called up for one of these honors *(aliyot).* Following the reading of the entire *Sedrah* (weekly Torah portion), the *Maftir* (the person who is to read the *Haftorah)* is called up. This is considered a special honor.

The *Maftir* portion consists of the repetition of the last three or more sentences of the *Sedrah.* You may possibly be asked to chant the *Maftir* when you are called up. After the Torah has been rolled up, raised, tied, and its cover replaced, the *Haftorah* is chanted.

When you have read the *Haftorah*, there are a few other prayers, and then the Torah is returned to the Ark. At this point of the service the rabbi usually gives his sermon, and you may also be requested to speak.

In your talk you could mention what your Bar Mitzvah means to you. You may discuss some of the contents of the day's *Sedrah* or *Haftorah* that are relevant to your Bar Mitzvah.

Whatever you say, your speech will have meaning and value only if it is delivered in your own words, on a topic that you yourself understand, and which you can deliver sincerely and naturally.

Then comes the *Musaf* ("additional") service, after which there usually follows a *Kiddush* (reception) that your parents have prepared in your honor.

THOUGHTS FOR AFTER
THE BAR MITZVAH

The ceremony and the reception following it have passed over well. You have enjoyed the special attention given you, and all the celebrations that have gone into your Bar Mitzvah. But now what?

One of the first things to ask yourself is: Has this entire celebration actually made me an adult Jew? As far as others are concerned, you are now considered to be a man, with all the rights and privileges to which having reached the age of Bar Mitzvah entitles you.

But if you are honest, you must admit that you really are inexperienced and know too little about your Judaism to be considered an adult Jew.

Then what has all this celebration been about? The Bar Mitzvah festivities seem to have more to do with what you are expected to do as you grow up than with anything you have learned so far. They are a kind of advance payment on your future. The question is: What kind of a future should that be in order to live up to all these expectations?

To enable you to live a full adult Jewish life, you should

1) continue with your Jewish studies so that you know what is expected of you as an adult and a Jew;

2) take these duties and responsibilities and put what you have learned into practice. Some of these new obligations include:

a) Praying every day of the year, including Sabbaths and festivals. Now that you may be counted as part of a *minyan* (ten or more men), it is up to you to make use of that privilege as often as you can.

b) Wearing the *tallit* and *tefillin* regularly as commanded. (The chapter "Tallit and Tefillin" offers a full discussion of these sacred objects.)

c) Observing the Sabbath, Dietary Laws, and other basic aspects of Jewish life.

d) Certain additional obligations that you owe to yourself, to your family, to your school and to your synagogue, to the Jewish community in your city, and to all Jews everywhere. For instance, you owe it to yourself to take part in Jewish social life. As for your family, you should respect your father, mother, grandparents, and other members of your family, and be helpful to your brothers and sisters when necessary. Where your school and synagogue are concerned, you ought to continue your Jewish education and take part in the activities of these institutions. You should also contribute as much

Bar Mitzvah observed at the Western Wall in Jerusalem.

as you can afford to Jewish welfare and charity work, show an interest in the affairs of Jews the world over, especially in Israel, and help with volunteer work in Jewish organizations.

3) make use of all your new rights and privileges.

These include your right to be counted as one of ten men required for a *minyan*, your right to be called to the Torah for an *aliyah*, and your right to lead a service in the synagogue, if you are able. Also, if you know how to chant the actual Torah reading before the congregation, you may well volunteer for this. If you are a Kohen, you are given the honor of blessing the congregation during the festival service. Also, you may be called upon to appear as a witness before the rabbinical court. But all of these privileges will be of value to you only if you make full use of them by regular attendance at synagogue services, by putting on *tallit* and *tefillin*, and by continuing your Hebrew studies, as well as by generally maintaining an interest in the life of the community. As you grow older and exercise your new privileges, you will become the kind of Jew you would like to be. This is a goal worth striving for.

41

ONE WAY OF PUTTING YOUR BAR MITZVAH
INSTRUCTION TO WORK

While you were preparing for your Bar Mitzvah ceremony, you probably put a great deal of effort into learning the special *Haftorah*, the *Maftir*, the blessings for the Torah and *Haftorah*, the laws of *tallit* and *tefillin*, and many other things. Perhaps you felt that all this was merely a rehearsal for a short ceremony that, after it was all over, would no longer be of any further value to you. If this is in fact what you thought, then you were completely mistaken.

In the first place, even if you have mastered only your own *Haftorah* and *Maftir* portions, you can still take pride in the fact that you already know that much. To know any of the Bible in its original Hebrew is something of an achievement! But you need not stop there. You should look on all the effort you put into your learning for your Bar Mitzvah as a preparation for further studies. Now that you know one *Haftorah*, you have the basis for learning others and understanding the message of the Prophets from which they are taken. If you see your Bar Mitzvah only as a beginning, you will constantly be enriching your Jewish knowlege.

When you were studying your *Haftorah*, you had to master not only the words but also the marks of musical recitation known as the *Trop*. Even if at the beginning you didn't learn them all, you could not help but become familiar with those recurring often enough in the course of the *Haftorah*.

Just as the eight notes of the scale are used in most Western music, and not only in one particular piece, so the accents of the Torah reappear in nearly every *Haftorah*, and not just in the one you learned. Therefore, using the knowledge of your *Haftorah* as a basis, and with a little practice, you will soon be able to sing any other *Haftorah* as well. These habits and skills, once acquired through your involvement with your own *Haftorah*, will come to your aid and make it easier for you to learn the next one, until, after building up a small repertoire, you will be able to read any *Haftorah* with little effort.

You will also find that many of the words, phrases, and expressions contained in your *Haftorah* will also recur in each new one you tackle.

Furthermore, from the *Haftorah* translation you may also have gained a general idea as to its contents. With each new portion that you learn, you will increase your knowledge of the inspired writings of the Prophets, and your knowledge of Hebrew will improve as well.

In addition, you will also have made yourself eligible to be called upon at any time for the *Haftorah* reading and for *Maftir*, the most highly sought-after of all the *aliyot*.

And, if you are capable of learning to read any *Haftorah*, you can use the same method to enable you to read any *Sedrah*, by using your present knowledge as a basis for learning other Torah portions as well. There is no end to the advantages you will reap from the knowledge

Bar Mitzvah speech, by Moritz Oppenheim, Germany, 19th century.

you have gained in preparing for your Bar Mitzvah. All this is true, of course, only on condition that you continue your Hebrew studies after your Bar Mitzvah.

This same method can also be applied to what you have learned from the use of your *tallit* and *tefillin*. Thus, the quotations from the Torah that are to be found in the prayers recited before and after putting on the *tallit* and *tefillin* will also make you familiar with some significant passages from our Torah. These few selections can then enable you to understand other similar Torah portions, including some of the basic laws and *mitzvot*.

Also, the portion you say after putting on your *tefillin*, taken from Exodus 13:1-16, acquaints you with some of the earliest laws of Passover. This passage, in turn, can then serve as an excellent model for understanding many other comparable passages taken from the Torah.

One piece of knowledge builds upon the next, just as one brick lays the foundation for another in the construction of a building. So, if you continue your Jewish studies after your Bar Mitzvah, all the hard work you have put into your learning for that occasion will help to make your Jewish studies that much easier for you in the future.

As a result of what's been said so far, I take it that you will now appreciate why your becoming Bar Mitzvah is merely the beginning of your Jewish education and not the end. The little that you have learned to become Bar Mitzvah can only help to put you on the road to greater and richer Jewish learning.

The growing movement for equal rights for women has in recent years led in many synagogues to the rise of the Bat Mitzvah ceremony for girls, intended as somewhat the equivalent of a boy's Bar Mitzvah. The purpose of this ceremony is to make a twelve-year-old girl feel as much aware of her responsibility toward her role in Jewish life as Bar Mitzvah does for a boy.

Now, even though the Bat Mitzvah ceremony differs widely from synagogue to synagogue and at present has no set form or tradition, it is usually understood that the girl must have some Hebrew knowledge and background, and that she must therefore prepare herself properly for the occasion.

The Jewish woman today, as in the ages past, must be prepared to join with her fellow Jews to keep our people alive. Both the Jewish man and the Jewish woman must act together in their respective roles. Each one has his or her duties to perform. Becoming Bat Mitzvah should enable the Jewish girl to become fully aware of her particular responsibility. Whether or not her reaching maturity is marked by a specific ceremony, the Jewish woman should keep these thoughts in mind to guide her through her life as a member of our people.*

*For more material on the role and preparation for Bat Mitzvah, read Sussman and Segal, *A Guide for Jewish Youth*, pp. 156-172.

TALLIT AND TEFILLIN

When you walk along the street, you hardly notice any difference in outward appearance between Jews and other people, but in the synagogue, the Jew is distinguished by his "Jewish uniform" — his *tallit* and *tefillin*.

A uniform indicates what the wearer does or is and how he is different from anyone else. For instance, a soldier's uniform tells us that the soldier's job is to protect his country, and a policeman's uniform tells us that the duty of the policeman is to keep law and order. A doctor's uniform or that of a nurse tells us that he or she cares for the sick . . . and the same formula applies to the uniform of a Jew. The *tallit* and *tefillin* reveal a Jew's pride in what he is and that his job is to carry out the commandments of the Torah.

In this chapter, I would like to deal with the question of what, exactly, the *tallit* and *tefillin* are, and to go more deeply into why we wear them. By putting them to daily use, you will soon see how the *tallit* and *tefillin* can enrich your enjoyment of Judaism.

WHAT THEY ARE

A *tallit* is worn during prayer every day of the year. It consists of an oblong piece of cloth woven from silk or wool and worn over the shoulders. Because of the *tzitzit*, the fringes that are attached to each of the four corners, the *tallit* is considered a holy garment. Each *tzitzit* contains four double threads, making eight in all, and five knots.

Although a *tallit* may be of either silk or wool, the main part of the garment, or *beged*, and each of the fringes must be made of the same material, based on the Torah prohibition not to wear flax and wool together.

A special blessing is recited before the *tallit* is put on. In addition to the *tallit*, Jewish men and boys also wear a *tallit katan*, or a "small *tallit*," which is a small four-cornered garment, also with four fringes, that fits over the shoulders but covers the chest and back as well. It is usually worn under the shirt, but not on the naked body, throughout the day.

Tefillin are used only on weekday mornings, never on Sabbaths or festivals.

There are two *tefillin*, one worn on the left arm and one on the head, just above the forehead. The *tefillin* worn on the arm is called the *shel yad* ("for the hand"), and the one on the head is the *shel rosh* ("for the head").

Each of the *tefillin* consists of a small black box with straps attached. In each box there is some parchment on which are written the four chapters from the Torah that command us to use *tefillin*. It is these sacred words written on the parchment (the material used instead of paper for *tefillin*, just as for a Torah scroll) that give *tefillin* their holiness.

The only difference between the parchments of the *shel yad* and the *shel rosh* is that in the latter each chapter is written on a separate piece and placed in a separate compartment, while in the *shel yad* all four chapters are written on a single piece of parchment and placed in one compartment.

WHY WE WEAR TALLIT AND TEFILLIN

The wearing of the *tallit* and *tefillin* is a commandment in the Torah, and whether we understand the reason for a *mitzvah* or not, we know that it is always for our ultimate good. However, the Torah does give us some of the reasons for this particular commandment.

As you go about your daily activities — school, work and recreation — you may at times forget that the laws of the Torah should be put into practice, not simply thought of or talked about. It therefore becomes necessary to have some constant physical reminder of our Torah, something that we can see and feel. The *tallit* and *tefillin* fulfill this purpose whenever you look at them and whenever you feel them touching your body.

Tefillin also remind us of our history and of our need to keep the chain of Jewish tradition strong and unbroken. As each Jew wears his *tallit* and *tefillin*, he not only strengthens his own individual link with Judaism but also serves as a source of encouragement for his fellow Jews to do the same.

When you are wearing your *tallit* and *tefillin*, you will feel properly dressed for prayer and in the proper mood to pray to God.

Only men wear a *tallit* and *tefillin*. Because a woman's chief responsibility in Jewish life is to her home and family, she is not required to keep any positive commandment that is to be observed at a specific time, as her attention might be demanded elsewhere. Since the *tallit* is worn only in the morning, when, according to the Bible, you "shall look at the *tzitzit*," this *mitzvah* is to be performed at a set time — that is, when it is already day-light. *Tefillin*, too, are worn only during the fixed times of prayer. Thus, since both of these *mitzvot* are dependent upon time, women are exempt from them.

WHY DO WE WEAR THE TALLIT?

To understand why we wear the *tallit*, we should look at the section in the Torah dealing with this *mitzvah* (Numbers 15:37-41):

"And the Lord spoke to Moses, saying: Speak to the Children of Israel, and tell them to make fringes on the corners of their garments throughout their generations, putting on the fringes of each corner a thread of blue. And it shall be to you for a fringe, so that you may look at it and remember all the commandments of the Lord, and do them; and so that you do not go astray after your own heart and your own eyes, which you use to go astray; so that you may remember to do all My commandments and be holy to your God; I am the Lord your God, Who brought you out of the land of Egypt to be your God; I am the Lord your God."

The emphasis here is placed on the *tzitzit* (fringes). When we look at them, we remind ourselves of certain basic principles:

1) All the 613 commandments of the Torah are holy, and we must keep as many of them as apply to us.
2) We must try not to break any of the laws and never be tempted away from the path of righteousness.

"Blessing of the Etrog," painting by Leopold Pilichowski.

Prayer shawl.

3) By keeping God's laws, we ourselves become holy and dedicate ourselves to God.
4) The *tallit* and *tefillin* remind us that God brought our ancestors out of Egypt so that we could become a nation dedicated to His service.

When we wear a *tallit* during prayer, we automatically show our love and respect for our Torah and its teachings.

If by wearing a *tallit* regularly during services we show respect for the *mitzvot*, how much more is this the case when we wear the *tallit katan* under our shirt the whole day long, and how much more do we thus set an example for others to be continually surrounded by *mitzvot*.

WHY ARE THE TEFILLIN WORN?

The *tefillin shel rosh* contains four different compartments with a separate one for each chapter on *tefillin*, while the *shel yad* contains all four chapters written on a single piece of parchment and placed in one compartment. This shows that although your mind (head) may be preoccupied with many things, action (hand) must come forth as a unified force.

The contents of the four chapters are:
1) Exodus 13:1-10. It is our duty to fulfill God's commandments.
2) Exodus 13:11-16. He freed us from Egypt and promised to give us the Holy Land.
3) Deuteronomy 6:4-9. God is One; we must love Him and observe His commandments at all times.

48

ארבע פרשיות התפילין

וידבר יהוה אל משה לאמר קדש לי כל בכור פטר כל רחם בבני ישראל באדם ובבהמה לי הוא ויאמר משה אל העם זכור את היום הזה אשר יצאתם ממצרים מבית עבדים כי בחזק יד הוציא יהוה אתכם מזה ולא יאכל חמץ היום אתם יצאים בחדש האביב והיה כי יביאך יהוה אל ארץ הכנעני והחתי והאמרי והחוי והיבוסי אשר נשבע לאבתיך לתת לך ארץ זבת חלב ודבש ועבדת את העבדה הזאת בחדש הזה שבעת ימים תאכל מצת וביום השביעי חג ליהוה מצות יאכל את שבעת הימים ולא יראה לך חמץ ולא יראה לך שאר בכל גבלך והגדת לבנך ביום ההוא לאמר בעבור זה עשה יהוה לי בצאתי ממצרים והיה לך לאות על ידך ולזכרון בין עיניך למען תהיה תורת יהוה בפיך כי ביד חזקה הוצאך יהוה ממצרים ושמרת את החקה הזאת למועדה מימים ימימה　　　והיה כי יבאך יהוה אל ארץ הכנעני כאשר נשבע לך ולאבתיך ונתנה לך והעברת כל פטר רחם ליהוה וכל פטר שגר בהמה אשר יהיה לך הזכרים ליהוה וכל פטר חמר תפדה בשה ואם לא תפדה וערפתו וכל בכור אדם בבניך תפדה והיה כי ישאלך בנך מחר לאמר מה זאת ואמרת אליו בחזק יד הוציאנו יהוה ממצרים מבית עבדים ויהי כי הקשה פרעה לשלחנו ויהרג יהוה כל בכור בארץ מצרים מבכר אדם ועד בכור בהמה על כן אני זבח ליהוה כל פטר רחם הזכרים וכל בכור בני אפדה והיה לאות על ידכה ולטוטפת בין עיניך כי בחזק יד הוציאנו יהוה ממצרים

שמע ישראל יהוה אלהינו יהוה אחד ואהבת את יהוה אלהיך בכל לבבך ובכל נפשך ובכל מאדך והיו הדברים האלה אשר אנכי מצוך היום על לבבך ושננתם לבניך ודברת בם בשבתך בביתך ובלכתך בדרך ובשכבך ובקומך וקשרתם לאות על ידך והיו לטטפת בין עיניך וכתבתם על מזזות ביתך ובשעריך　　　והיה אם שמע תשמעו אל מצותי אשר אנכי מצוה אתכם היום לאהבה את יהוה אלהיכם ולעבדו בכל לבבכם ובכל נפשכם ונתתי מטר ארצכם בעתו יורה ומלקוש ואספת דגנך ותירשך ויצהרך ונתתי עשב בשדך לבהמתך ואכלת ושבעת השמרו לכם פן יפתה לבבכם וסרתם ועבדתם אלהים אחרים והשתחויתם להם וחרה אף יהוה בכם ועצר את השמים ולא יהיה מטר והאדמה לא תתן את יבולה ואבדתם מהרה מעל הארץ הטבה אשר יהוה נתן לכם ושמתם את דברי אלה על לבבכם ועל נפשכם וקשרתם אתם לאות על ידכם והיו לטוטפת בין עיניכם ולמדתם אתם את בניכם לדבר בם בשבתך בביתך ובלכתך בדרך ובשכבך ובקומך וכתבתם על מזוזות ביתך ובשעריך למען ירבו ימיכם וימי בניכם על האדמה אשר נשבע יהוה לאבתיכם לתת להם כימי השמים על הארץ

The four sections of the Torah that are placed
within the tefillin (phylacteries).

49

4) Deuteronomy 11:13-21. God rewards us if we obey His commandments and punishes us if we disobey them.

Since these ideas form the very basis of Judaism, we must call them to mind every day by wearing the *tefillin*. These sections also remind us to study the Torah continually.

Before a boy is 13, he is not required to put on *tefillin* (except during the month or so before his Bar Mitzvah, when he begins to practice using them). Wearing *tefillin*, then, is a sign of Jewish manhood. It is one of the major responsibilities a Jewish boy takes upon himself when he makes the transition from childhood to becoming an adult. In other words, the *tefillin* are the Jewish symbol most closely associated with becoming Bar Mitzvah, or of age as a Jew.

HOW ARE THEY WORN?

A *tallit* should be worn every morning during the year (except on the Fast of *Av*) so that the *tzitzit* are visible by daylight. The *tallit* is also worn on *Yom Kippur* night, although it is put on while there is still light. For this one time during the year we wear it at night as a reminder that during the whole of *Yom Kippur* we are all regarded before God as His angels, thanks to the glory and splendor that the *tallit* symbolizes.

The *tefillin*, on the other hand, are worn on weekdays only, as a sign of God's covenant with Israel. On Sabbaths and festivals no such sign is necessary, because the very holiness of those particular days serves as a reminder. In fact, according to some views, if we should wear the *tefillin* on those days, this could be taken as an insult to their holiness, since we need no extra reminder of God's closeness to Israel. Also, strange as it may seem, we are even forbidden to touch the *tefillin* on these holy days.

During the middle days (*Hol ha-Moed*) of Passover and *Sukkot*, *tefillin* are worn in some congregations and not in others. It is usual to follow the practice of the particular congregation where you are praying.

On the Fast of *Av* (the saddest day in our calendar) *tefillin* are worn during the afternoon service instead of in the morning. Just as a mourner is exempt from wearing *tefillin* before the burial of a loved one, so on this day, when we mourn the loss of our Temple (as well as all the other tragedies that occurred on that day), we are not likely to be in the right mood to concentrate on prayer. What is more, the *tefillin* serve as a kind of badge or decoration. During such a period of mourning, a person certainly does not feel like wearing any sort of ornament.

After making the appropriate blessing, the *tallit* is put on. Immediately thereafter, as the *tefillin* are being donned, two separate blessings (one for the *shel yad* and one for the *shel rosh*) are said. The *tallit* is put on before the *tefillin* because, as indicated before, it is used more often.

Bag for prayer shawl, Morocco, 19th century.
Prayer book in silver binding, Italy, 17th century.

PUTTING ON THE TALLIT

We put on the *tallit* in the following way. As we stand holding it in front of us, we say the blessing; then we kiss the *tzitzit* and place the *tallit* over the shoulders. If it is a full-length *tallit*, we wrap the garment over the head, as a customary symbol of enwrapping ourselves in God's holiness. We then recite a short prayer while still wearing it.

Before putting on the *tallit katan* in the morning, we first recite the blessing *al mitzvat tzitzit* and then kiss the *tzitzit*. The garment is worn under the shirt, but is never directly in contact with the body.

During the reading of the *Shema* in the morning, the four fringes are held together in one hand, and each time you come to the word *tzitzit* in the third paragraph of the *Shema*, you kiss them. This custom makes the words come alive and is at the same time a sign of respect and love.

Should the threads of the *tzitzit* become torn or damaged, they must be replaced; neither the regular *tallit* nor the *tallit katan* may be used unless all four *tzitzit* are in the proper condition.

PUTTING ON THE TEFILLIN

Just as with the *tallit*, the *tefillin* are put on while standing. First, the *shel yad* is placed on the biceps of the upper left arm (since this is the one closest to the heart),* followed by the recitation of the first blessing for putting on the *tefillin*. The strap *(retzuah)* is wound around the lower arm seven times. Then the *shel rosh* is placed on the head, just above the forehead, and the second blessing, *al mitzvat tefillin*, is recited. Another line, *barukh Shem k'vod . . .* follows. Finally, as the strap of the *shel yad* of the left hand is wound around the fingers and the palm of the left hand to form the letter *shin*, the verses *ve-ay-ras-tikh li* are recited.**

The Hebrew word *Shaddai*, a Name of God, is formed from the *shin* made on the back of the hand (this letter is also engraved on the side of the *shel rosh);* from the *daled* which is the shape of the knot of the *shel rosh;* and from the *yod*, which is the shape of the knot of the *shel yad*, serving as a reminder of the Divine Name.

The recitation of the morning prayers then follows.

The *tefillin* are removed in the reverse order from that in which they are put on. Thus, the *shin* formed on the hand is first undone; then comes the *shel rosh* and, finally, the *shel yad*. There is no special way of putting away *tefillin*, but they must be returned to the *tefillin* bag in good order.

Tefillin should be examined every few years by an expert *sofer* (Hebrew scribe) to insure that the parchment, the writing, and all the other parts are still in good and usable condition.

Because of their great sanctity and significance, the *tefillin* are to be handled with the utmost care and respect.

THE TALLIT AND TEFILLIN HABIT

Just as you are accustomed to praying every day, so should you get into the habit of wearing *tallit* and *tefillin* on the applicable days, before your breakfast and other daily activities. Even if you have to miss praying in the synagogue with a *minyan* (quorum of ten adult males), *tallit* and *tefillin* may still be worn when praying at home.

---

*A man who is left-handed may be required to put the *shel-yad* on his right arm and should consult a rabbi.
**For more detailed information and diagrams, see H.H. Donin, *To Be A Jew*, pp. 146-160.

Like any other habit, the wearing of *tallit* and *tefillin* will grow on you. Soon, not wearing your *tefillin* when you should will make you feel improperly dressed, as though you were clothed in but half a uniform.

The regular wearing of *tefillin* shows that one is capable of action, rather than just talking about, thinking of, and believing in Judaism.

SOME VALUES OF THE "TALLIT AND TEFILLIN HABIT"

The *tallit* and *tefillin* always remind us of what it means to be a Jew and of the type of life a Jew should lead.

The wearing of *tallit* and *tefillin* fills the Jew with a special sense of pride, since his is a type of uniform signifying both that he is in God's service and that he is observing a commandment thousands of years old.

Also, when another Jew sees you in your *tallit* and *tefillin*, this in itself encourages him, too, to wear them, and will bring you that much closer to your fellow Jew. Since you will actually be wearing on your body texts from the holy Torah, you will be brought that much closer to the spirit of the Torah as well.

The wearing of *tefillin* also serves to strengthen the Jewish future. When you grow up and have a family, when your son sees you in your *tallit* and *tefillin*, he will naturally want to follow your example. Your daughter will also respect you for this, and when she too has children, she will encourage them to follow the example she has learned from you.

The inner happiness that you will receive by these "signs" will be with you forever and will enrich your enjoyment of Judaism.

WHY JEWS WEAR A HEAD COVERING

Jews wear a head covering to show the world that they are Jewish.

Even though this practice has not been commanded in the Torah, it has developed among Jews as a sign of respect and of their belief in God. The Torah tells us not to be like those non-Jews who do not believe in God (Leviticus 18:3) but, rather, to follow the laws of our Torah.

During Roman times the wearing of a head covering was a sign of disgrace, because only a slave had to cover his head. A free man went bareheaded. In order to demonstrate that we were the servants of God, Jews would cover their heads in the synagogue in prayer, or whenever God's name was mentioned. Later it became the practice to wear a head covering all the time out of respect for God. "Cover your head, so that the fear of Heaven will be upon you" (*Shabbat* 156b).

As you can see, the wearing of a head covering has become both a sign of respect for God and a means of telling the world that one is a Jew and that he respects the traditions of his people. It reminds us that, as Jews, we are different from others in that we have something special to offer — including a religion that has become a mother to at least two others, and a way of living that other peoples have imitated.

The head covering, then, has evolved into something of a national and religious symbol; it represents what is unique and special in Judaism, both as a religion and as a way of life, and should therefore become your badge of honor.

The most common form of head covering, especially that worn indoors, is the skullcap, known in Yiddish as a *yarmulke* and in Hebrew as a *kippah*. As a special type of head covering, the *yarmulke* in itself has no religious significance but is worn in place of a hat, primarily for comfort and convenience. It can be found in a variety of styles and colors and is often artistically decorated.

Mosaic floor of the synagogue of Beth Alpha
in the Valley of Jezreel. The mosaic floor was
laid according to an inscription in the days of
the Byzantine emperor Justin I (518-527).

THE SYNAGOGUE IN JEWISH LIFE

INTRODUCTION:

THE SYNAGOGUE, THE JEW'S "SECOND HOME"

Do you know that in addition to the home where you live, you
also have a "second home"? A home you don't have to rent or buy, but
one where you will always find other Jews who share it with you? That
home is the synagogue.

Why is it a second home for you? Simply because that is where
you belong whenever you are not in your own home. And why do you

belong there? Because you are a Jew, and a Jew cannot do without his or her synagogue. He needs it for a few reasons, not simply for prayer alone, and these reasons will be discussed shortly. It is in the synagogue that he is made to feel comfortable and at ease. Just how and why every Jewish person should feel at home in this "second home" of his will be explained during the course of this chapter.

Have you ever been to a synagogue? If you haven't, you should go. Not just for a casual visit now and then, but as the place where you belong every day of the year.

In case you have visited a synagogue (as you most likely have), did you feel at home there? If you did, then the material in this chapter will have some real meaning for you. But if the synagogue did not seem like home to you at that time, then I am certain that much of what you will learn about it here will help you feel more at home the next time you go there.

In fact, this knowledge about the synagogue will prove beneficial to you not merely by making you feel more comfortable there but also for many of the interesting things that you will learn. (Read or review the chapter in this book on "Prayer and Worship.")

WHAT IS A SYNAGOGUE?

Almost every religion has a special place where people come together to worship and to pray. The Christians have their church and the Moslems their mosque. But did you know that both the Christians and the Moslems first learned about having a place of worship from the Jewish synagogue?

The basic definition of a synagogue is a place set aside for prayer. However, to us Jews a synagogue is something more than merely a place in which to pray. It is where we Jews gather for the three different purposes it provides: a *Bet Tefillah* (House of Prayer), a *Bet ha-Midrash* (House of Study), and a *Bet ha-Knesset* (House of Coming Together).

Throughout most of this chapter I will try to show you just how the synagogue fulfills each one of these three functions. It is in these three ways that the synagogue has served the Jew throughout the greater part of our history — that is, as a place where Jews come together to worship; where they study and learn, both during their prayer services and before and after worship; and where they gather on important occasions in their lives, such as a wedding, a Bar Mitzvah, a *Brit Milah*, and the like.

Because of these three functions, the Jew can easily feel at home in his synagogue. That may be one reason why the Hebrew word *bet* (meaning a "house" or a "home") is used to describe the ways in which the synagogue serves the Jew.

In the pages that follow, you will be shown just what each of these three functions means to the Jew.

Synagogue in Worms, Germany. The smaller building is the "Rashi Chapel."

WHY DO WE NEED A SYNAGOGUE?

Has the above question ever entered your mind? You might have also wondered, "Of what good is it to us?" In case you have been puzzled by such questions, just remember that prayer is something vital in the life of every human being, providing a means of expressing one's feelings toward God. As a Jew, a person must have a synagogue as a place for prayer.

In that case you may then be asking, "But couldn't I pray just as well without a synagogue, any time or anywhere I feel like praying?" Perhaps yes. But please remind yourself of the differences between formal and informal prayer, as explained in the chapter on "Prayer and Worship."

There you were told that even though private or informal prayer is as acceptable to God as is formal prayer, it is when Jews gather together to pray as one that their prayers are most effective. In fact, our sages have told us that the verse from Psalms 16:8, "I have set the Lord before me always," is intended to teach us that every Jew should pray to God all the time. However, because this is not practical for most of us, inasmuch as we have to attend to our daily work or to school, our sages have instead commanded us to pray three times a day. For this purpose a synagogue is the only place where such regular worship can be achieved.

Furthermore, there are certain prayers that cannot be recited without a *minyan*. Also the Torah cannot be read unless a *minyan* is present. Thus, only a synagogue can fill this need for a place of prayer. Then again, remember that, as a central place where many Jews come together, the synagogue unites each Jew with every other Jew and makes them all feel as one before God.

57

One of the oldest European synagogues, established in the middle of the 14th century in Dubrovnik, Yugoslavia.

Synagogue in the Ukraine, 17th century.

Finally, it is only in a synagogue that its remaining two functions — as a House of Study and as a House of Coming Together — can find their true meaning.

As you will soon see, learning, in Jewish life, must take place along with prayer. This is true in the case of the reading of the Torah, as well as of certain portions of prayers which contain material to be learned and understood (see chapter on "Prayer"). Such a combination of learning and prayer is possible only in a synagogue.

However, we Jews not only pray and study, we also have occasion to come together for other activities: for happy events such as a wedding or a Bar Mitzvah, as well as, God forbid, times of sorrow, when all people share their feelings with the bereaved.

There are also study classes, social events, meetings, and celebrations — the many day-to-day activities — for which the synagogue is the most suitable place.

In short, we need a synagogue so that it can perform the three basic functions for which it was always meant — prayer, study, and social gathering. Or, to put it otherwise, even though a synagogue's functions must begin with prayer, they must not end there.

HOW DID THE SYNAGOGUE COME TO BE?

Before There Were Synagogues

The birth of the synagogue as a separate institution can be traced back to about the period following the destruction of the First Temple, which occurred in the year 586 B.C.E. From that time on, as we shall soon see, the synagogue grew in number and in importance.

But even before there was a synagogue, the Jews still had a place for prayer. Let us take a look at our early history to find out more.

The very earliest places of worship mentioned in the Bible were the altars that the patriarchs — Abraham, Isaac, and Jacob — built, and before which they expressed their feelings toward God. (Read about these altars in the Book of Genesis.)

Later, during the time of Moses, the Israelites built a Tabernacle, which was a sort of movable Temple, in which they worshipped during their wanderings through the desert. In this Tabernacle they would offer sacrifices of animals or offerings of meal and sing certain hymns while doing so. The Tabernacle was a holy place because the Two Tablets of the Law rested there in a Holy Ark. Certain other holy objects, such as a *Menorah* and altars, were also found in the Tabernacle.

This Tabernacle served as a moving Temple even after the Israelites had already entered the land of Canaan (Israel). Wherever it would be standing at any particular time would then become their central place of worship.

However, the Israelites were not satisfied with a roving Temple. They wanted a permanent one. Therefore, after King David had conquered Jerusalem and made it the center of the nation, his son, Solomon, built the First Temple. This structure was an object of art and beauty, and it became the permanent place to which Jews from everywhere could come to bring their sacrifices — there and nowhere else. Here all the sacrifices were offered by the priests as commanded by the Torah.

Then, on the sad day of the Ninth of Av *(Tisha b'Av)*, in the year 586 B.C.E., this lovely Temple was destroyed by the Babylonians, who had finally conquered the Jews following a bitter war.

The Earliest Synagogues

Most of the Jews were then led into exile in Babylonia, where they settled. However, after they realized that they could no longer worship in the Temple in Jerusalem, many of them met for prayer on Sabbaths and festivals in the homes of their prophets, who at that time served as their teachers. In this way did the idea of a synagogue gradually come into being. Here they also studied portions from the Torah and from other holy writings. Their prayers consisted largely of the *Shema*, the *Amidah*, and excerpts from the Psalms, as well as certain prayers which described the Temple sacrifices.

After the Temple was rebuilt in the year 516 B.C.E., the Jews still continued to worship in their synagogues. In fact, there was even a synagogue in the Temple, in the *Lishkat ha-Gazit* (Court of the Hewn Stone), where the Sanhedrin would meet.

Inasmuch as during the exile the Jews had studied the Torah and other holy writings, following the rebuilding of the Temple they now combined study with prayer. In this way it became customary to read the Torah a few times each week, just as we do now. Many of the prayers also contained portions for study. Also, certain Temple ceremonies were transferred to the synagogue, such as parading around the synagogue with the *lulav* and *etrog* on *Sukkot*, the blessing of the people by the priests, and others.

The Continued Growth of the Synagogue

Following the destruction of the Second Temple, in 70 C.E., the synagogue became even more important to the Jews because now it was their only place of worship. More prayers were added until, by the time of the Talmudic period (around 400 C.E. and after), most of the synagogue service as we know it today had already been established, and many new prayers have been added ever since. The synagogue grew in importance and continued to increase in number, both in Israel and in other lands. During the days of the Second Temple there were over four hundred synagogues in Jerusalem alone.

Also, just as the need for Jewish learning had grown during the period following the destruction of the Second Temple, in like manner did the role of the synagogue as a *Bet ha-Midrash* gain in importance. Thus, in addition to the study of the Bible, the regular study of the Talmud rose to a higher level in the synagogue. It had already become customary to set aside regular, definite times each day for Talmudic readings.

*Eternal Light,
U.S.A.
20th century.*

Prayer and study now became inseparable in the life of the synagogue. However, the synagogue's third function, as a *Bet ha-Knesset* (House of Assembly, or Community House), did not begin to achieve prominence until the period of the Middle Ages, even though this latter function had already existed during the earlier days of the synagogue.

It was during the Middle Ages — when many Jews were forced to live in ghettos — that the synagogue gradually evolved into a Jewish center, as well as a house of study and prayer. By that time it was common for Jews to gather there for occasions such as a *Brit Milah*, wedding, or a Bar Mitzvah celebration; to make public announcements of lost-and-found articles; to conduct a Jewish court; and, in times of trouble or danger, as a place of refuge. In addition to these functions, the synagogue also served as a place of shelter for travelers, students or beggars.

Most Jews lived close to the synagogue because hardly any part of the daily life of a Jew was separate from it. Thus, for the Jew of medieval and later times, the synagogue was truly his "second home."

The general pattern of the synagogue with its three functions has continued even until this day. However, some of its other purposes have changed since those earlier times. For example, the synagogue today is hardly ever used as a lodging place for travelers and others. Nor does a Jew come to his synagogue for lost-or-found articles.

Furthermore, as Jewish life in various countries developed, three different branches of Judaism arose: Orthodox, Conservative. and

Reform. These three groups will be discussed more fully later on in this chapter, when we will note the manner in which each division affected the nature and life of the synagogue.

A LOOK AT THE SYNAGOGUE —
INSIDE AND OUTSIDE

Our rabbis have called the synagogue a *mikdash me'at* (small sanctuary) because it had become the place of worship for the Jews (without sacrifices, of course) after the Temple in Jerusalem had been destroyed. However, because the Temple building had been considered by the Jews to be a most masterful object of art and beauty, they tried to make their synagogues as beautiful in appearance as they could afford to. It is for this reason that a synagogue today is usually a very attractive-looking structure. Since there is no set plan or design to which its exterior must adhere, the esthetic qualities of the building depend upon the wishes, tastes, and wealth of the congregation's members.

As you step inside a synagogue, you will notice many objects that are to be found in nearly every other synagogue. But of all these objects, there are two that every synagogue must have if it is to qualify as a *Bet Tefillah*. These are a *Holy Ark* and a *ner tamid* (eternal light), both of which were among the holy objects of the Temple of old.

While the Ark of the Temple had been a gold-lined chest containing the Two Tablets of the Law, the Holy Ark *(Aron ha-Kodesh)* of every synagogue is usually a built-in wall cabinet with doors, and in it are to be found the Torah scrolls *(Sifrei Torah)*. Without these Torah scrolls the synagogue is not considered to be a holy place.

Each Torah scroll consists of a long roll of hand-written parchment attached to two sticks (the *atzei ḥayyim*). The Torah is covered with a decorated velvet mantle, and over the *atzei ḥayyim* are hung a silver breastplate and a silver Torah pointer *(yad)*. (It is forbidden to touch the Torah parchment while it is being read.)

Eternal Light, Morocco 20th century.

Draped over the Ark is the *parokhet* (curtain), which is artistically decorated with Hebrew lettering and other designs. Above and slightly in front of the Ark hangs the *ner tamid*, a lamp which must burn continuously, just as it did in the Temple of old, as a sign of God's promise to Israel that He will always protect them as His people and will always love them.

In front of the Ark stands the *bimah* (platform), on which rests the *Shulḥan* (reading desk), from which the Torah is read. In the strictly Orthodox synagogues the *bimah* is placed in the center of the sanctuary.

Almost every synagogue has *Magen David* designs (six-pointed stars) on many of the holy objects just described. You will also find one or more *Menorot* (candelabras) beside or near the *Aron ha-Kodesh* or the *bimah*. The *Menorah* used today is a reminder of the one with seven branches that was present in the ancient Temple. However, in

*Torah Ark of Mantova-Sermide, Italy, 1543,
now in Israel.*

order to avoid giving it the same appearance, a six or eight branch *Menorah* is used instead.

Many synagogues have stained-glass windows with various designs and Hebrew lettering. Carvings and inscriptions might also be found on the synagogue walls, as might other forms of artistic paintings or decorations. As long as they are in keeping with Jewish law, the types of decorations will be decided by the members of the synagogue. Nevertheless, you will never find any pictures or forms of human figures in a synagogue, possibly because the Second Commandment forbids the making of any forms or images that might become objects of worship.

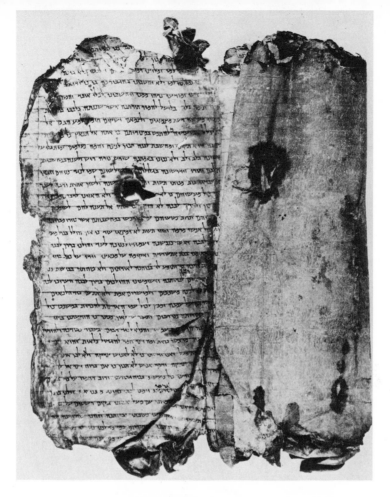

First sheet of the "Thanksgiving Scroll," one of the seven in possession of the Hebrew University of Jerusalem, partially unrolled.

In most Reform temples and in some that are Conservative, an organ is used during services. But the Orthodox forbid its use, especially because it serves as a reminder of the destruction of the Temple, where musical instruments had been played by the priests.

In Orthodox synagogues, men and women sit separately during services, divided by a *mehitzah* (divider). The *mehitzah* may be in the form of either a balcony or a mezzanine for the women's section, or else some other divider on the floor level. Such a division of men and women is required, based originally upon the *ezrat nashim* (women's section) that was used in the Temple in order to prevent any inappropriate conduct between the sexes during the services or festivities.

Another fundamental reason for the need of a *mehitzah* in a synagogue is that during worship, every person must be able to concentrate properly upon his or her prayers. And since human nature is such that a male and female tend to attract each other when together, the presence of a member of the opposite sex could easily prevent the worshipper from giving his or her full attention to the prayer.

63

Contrary to what has sometimes been suggested, the purpose of separate seating is definitely not meant to make the women feel inferior to the man. Just the opposite. By sitting apart from a man, a woman has the opportunity to be treated as man's equal, because she can concentrate on her prayers as well as a man can. She thereby performs her *mitzvah* of prayer in the same manner as a man does, and is thus treated as his equal, certainly not his inferior.

(For some additional explanations of the reasons for a *mehitzah*, read the article *Separate Pews in the Synagogue* by Norman Lamm, in J.B. Litwin's volume, *The Sanctity of the Synagogue.*)

WHAT ARE THE THREE MAIN
BRANCHES OF JUDAISM TODAY?

Up until about two hundred years ago most Jews throughout the world generally were traditional Jews; that is, they lived according to the laws of the Torah, even though there may have been many differences among them. Then, during the early nineteenth century, the Reform movement arose — a movement that observed Judaism quite differently from how it had been observed until that time. Later, during the same century, another group came into being — the Conservative movement. This group of Jews felt that the Reformers had strayed too far from traditional Judaism, and they therefore sought a middle path between the Orthodox (the strict, traditional Jews) and the former.

Many differences in observances developed among the three groups, although our discussion here will consider only those between each group's synagogues and then will compare the three of them.

ORTHODOX, CONSERVATIVE, AND REFORM
SYNAGOGUES TODAY

Let us now see how a synagogue of each of the above-mentioned three branches of Judaism — Orthodox, Conservative, Reform — serves as a House of Prayer, as a House of Study, and as a Community Center in today's world.

1) As a Bet Tefillah

In an Orthodox or Conservative synagogue, services are held daily — every morning, late afternoon, and early evening. A Reform temple generally holds its worship only on Sabbaths (especially Friday evening) and festivals.

In the Orthodox and Conservative synagogues men wear *talliyot* and worship with their heads covered, whereas these are not made requirements in a Reform temple. In all three types of synagogues the Torah is read on the Sabbath and festivals, and, in the Orthodox and Conservative synagogues, it is also read on Sabbath afternoon and on Monday and Thursday mornings.

Why must the Torah be read on Mondays and Thursdays as well

Prayers in the synagogue on the Feast of Tabernacles, etching, London, 1800. Scroll case, Iraq, 19th century.

as on the Sabbath? According to our rabbis, the Prophets had commanded that no three days in any week should ever go by without the Torah being read.

During the Torah service in all three congregations, the Ark is opened and the Torah scroll is removed and paraded around the synagogue amid special prayers. It is then opened and read by a special Torah reader, a *baal korei*. On the Sabbath seven or more men are called up for an *aliyah* (Torah honor) to recite the Torah blessings; six are called on *Yom Kippur*; five on festivals not falling on the Sabbath; four on *Rosh Ḥodesh* (New Moon); and three during the weekdays and on Sabbath afternoon.

The prayer services as outlined in the chapter on "Prayer" are recited for each service. In the Orthodox synagogues the "Priestly Blessing" service is added on festivals. (For an interesting description of this service, see H.H. Donin, *To Be A Jew*, pp. 198-206.)

Since weekday services are much shorter and much simpler than those for the Sabbath and festivals, they are usually held in a smaller room of the building, called a "daily chapel" or a "daily *Bet ha-Midrash*," the latter also being used for study purposes.

2) As a Bet ha-Midrash

Now, because prayer and study blend together so harmoniously in Jewish life, it is only natural that where we pray and study — in the synagogue — they also work together inseparably to build toward wholesome Jewish living. In fact, our rabbis have told us that in their days (nearly two thousand years ago) every one of the four hundred and eighty synagogues in Jerusalem had both an elementary school and a high school.

Let us therefore compare the manner in which each of the three branches of Judaism puts the principle of prayer and study into practice.

Whenever we hear the rabbi delivering his sermon or the Torah being read, we gain some learning from both these sources. However, in the Orthodox and Conservative congregations, additional Torah knowledge can be acquired through the groups in which many Jews study the Bible, Talmud, or other holy writings, either before or after services, between *minha* (afternoon) and *ma'ariv* (evening) services during weekdays, or on Sabbath afternoons.

In addition to these classes, the synagogue may sponsor other adult classes in which various courses such as Hebrew, Jewish history, Bible, Jewish literature, and the like, are taught. There may also be lectures on Jewish topics of interest, along with many other educational activities.

For the children and youth, most synagogues of today have a daily afternoon Hebrew school, and many of them, particularly the Conservative and Reform, provide a Sunday school as well. Some Orthodox synagogues also sponsor a *Yeshivah*, a school of intensive religious study, and many other Orthodox as well as some Conservative synagogues offer a Hebrew Day School.

As a general rule, most Reform temples have been known to conduct only a one-day-a-week school, usually on Sunday. However, during the past several years many Reform congregations have also required their students to attend on weekday afternoons. In fact, still more recently, some Reform synagogues have also organized Day Schools.

3) As a Bet ha-Knesset

Regarding this function, there appear to be the least number of differences between the three branches. All of them seek to bring their followers together for social purposes, even though, as has already been mentioned, the synagogue of today does not perform as many functions as it did centuries ago.

Yet every synagogue is known as the place for a Bar Mitzvah, a *Kiddush* following services, and meetings of religious organizations (Zionist groups, Sisterhoods and Men's Clubs, and the synagogue board of directors). Concerts and social affairs of all kinds are held in the synagogue; it is also the place for a community *Seder*, a *Purim* carnival, and a *Ḥanukkah* party. In addition, the synagogue helps raise funds for many local, national, and world organizations, such as those for Israel, for its local Jewish Welfare Fund, for the United Jewish Appeal, and for countless others.

Through these three basic functions — prayer, study, and social activities — the synagogue fills many vital needs for our Jewish people. They help us to understand why a Jew has always become part of the synagogue; it is his "second home" and is where he belongs.

WHO SERVES IN A SYNAGOGUE?

It may seem surprising, but the synagogue of today requires very few full-time workers to serve it. In earlier times, as we shall soon see, even fewer regular employees did the work of serving and maintaining the synagogue. However, as small a number as they really are, those who do conduct the work of the congregation must be highly qualified and very responsible individuals, in order that the synagogue function properly.

The Rabbi

The term "rabbi" has quite a different meaning today than it once had. Up until about five hundred years ago, a rabbi was meant to be only a scholar and a teacher. He was not connected with any synagogue and would earn his livelihood from some other occupation. We therefore hear of great rabbis of ancient times (and later) working as physicians, farmers, merchants, artists, skilled laborers, and so forth.

However, with changed conditions and with the need for a rabbi to devote his full time to a congregation, it was later found necessary to pay the rabbi a salary for his time and his professional efforts.

During the past few hundred years a rabbi often served as the spiritual leader of an entire Jewish community, rather than of any one synagogue. He was considered to be the chief authority on Jewish law and practice, and his word commanded the highest respect of that community.

In like manner does today's rabbi usually serve his congregation. In order to qualify for such a highly responsible position, he must be, first and foremost, a man of unquestionable character and a fully observant Jew. He must be deeply learned in Torah, Talmud, Jewish law, and, in fact, as many other branches of Jewish knowledge as possible.

As evidence of his having devoted the necessary years of study to all the required subjects and of his being fully proficient in them, he must possess a *semikhah*, a certificate of ordination, either from a well-recognized *Yeshivah* or from an outstanding rabbinical authority.

In line with his title of rabbi or *rav* (teacher), he must be able to teach Torah to his followers in various ways, through his sermons, as well as in the classes he will conduct. In many cases the rabbi will be called upon to answer questions concerning Jewish law and to serve as judge in disputes which may arise. For all of these functions he must have a sound knowledge of Jewish law.

In addition to requiring a man with profound Jewish learning, many congregations seek a rabbi who also has a solid background in the area of general worldly knowledge. As the spiritual leader of his congregation, the rabbi must likewise possess the qualities of one who will command the respect and earn the love of his congregation and his community.

These are but a few of the many qualifications and duties which are required of a rabbi and which, to some extent, may vary from one congregation to another. As a rule, the success of a congregation will often depend upon the kind of leadership given to it by its rabbi.

The Cantor

An even greater change has taken place in the position of a cantor (or, *hazzan*) from what it had been during the days of the Talmud, about two thousand years ago. At that time the duties of a *hazzan* were similar to those of today's *shammash* (sexton). The modern cantor serves as the congregation's spokesman before God, or, as the *shaliah tzibbur*. It is he who leads the prayer service which he chants.

In addition to a pleasing voice and musical ability, the *hazzan* must also possess certain other qualities, a few of which follow:

a) Like the rabbi, his moral character and observance of the *mitzvot* must be beyond question.

b) He must be a person who is acceptable to his congregation and who has their love and respect.

c) He must have an understanding of the prayers he is chanting. In fact, knowing the meaning of the prayers is considered to be much more important than having a beautiful singing voice.

d) He must be familiar with traditional melodies that are suitable for different services.

e) The cantor must also have an understanding of Jewish life and be able to participate in matters of interest to the Jewish community.

As a rule, the cantor is likely to be in charge of most of the musical activities connected with the synagogue, such as his choir and other choral groups of the synagogue and school. He will also assist the rabbi at weddings, funerals, or other such occasions where his chanting is called for.

He may, in addition, perform other needed functions around the synagogue. Whenever the cantor is absent from Sabbath or weekday services, any man who can do so will conduct the services as *shaliah tzibbur*.

Scroll case, Iraq, 19th century.

Inasmuch as Jews often object to a cantor who prolongs the service with unnecessarily drawn-out melodies, he will generally be more popular with his congregants if he heeds this caution.

The Sexton *(Shammash)*

The sexton usually has quite a variety of duties to perform. It is he who often supervises the daily services and who looks after the *Siddurim, Ḥumashim* (Bibles), *talliyot,* and other religious articles, seeing that they are in proper condition and in place. In the absence of the cantor, he may be called upon to chant the services, or even to read the Torah. At times he will also assist the rabbi in various ways.

Even though he is not expected to possess more learning than any other educated Jew, or to have any special knowledge for his work, he should still be an observant Jew and one whose education compares well with that of other learned Jews. Therefore, the more proficient he is in Jewish studies and the more capable he is in the work necessary around the synagogue, the more tasks and responsibilities will be given to him to perform.

The *Gabbai*

This term, as used today, refers to the man in charge of directing the functioning of the synagogue services from day to day. He is the one who usually assigns various duties to the laymen, such as serving as cantor or Torah reader, determines the time of each service, and also gives out the Torah honors, such as *aliyot,* lifting the Torah, and opening the Ark. The *gabbai* also supervises the work of the *shammash.*

During the earliest days of the synagogue its only two regular officials were the *shammash* and the *gabbai.* All other duties were performed by men from among the congregants. But today the term *gabbai* can also include the president of the congregation, who works with the other officers and the board of directors in handling the general government of the synagogue, especially its financial affairs, as well as any other matters that concern its general welfare.

69

Synagogue of Carpentras, France, built in the 14th century, reconstructed in the 18th century.

HOW DOES THE ORGANIZATION OF
A SYNAGOGUE FUNCTION TODAY?

Earlier you were shown how the synagogue of today functions as a House of Prayer, a House of Study and a Social Center. But let us now examine the workings of a synagogue as an organization.

According to the definition of a synagogue as stated above, it is any room or building which is set aside for prayer. From this definition you can see that even though a synagogue performs the three general functions already discussed, it must start out as a House of Prayer. Its functions as a House of Study and as a Community House usually come later.

By its being a House of Prayer, it must have no less than ten adult male members — a *minyan* — and must conform to the Jewish Codes of Law. From then on, it is a self-governing organization that decides for itself just how the congregation is to function. It is, then, a completely independent organization.

With these few facts in mind, let us now see just how a synagogue gets started and comes into being. Even though all synagogues may or may not follow the steps outlined below, most houses of worship have been formed along these general lines.

Let us say that in a certain locality ten or more Jewish males aged thirteen or over wish to organize themselves into a synagogue. Their first step must be to find a place for holding worship services. This place can be any room, public hall, or building which is fit for becoming a synagogue. No doubt the great majority of synagogues today held their first services either in a private home, a rented storeroom, or some other such location.

The new synagogue must next acquire at least one *Sefer Torah* scroll, prayer books, Bibles, *talliyot*, and whatever other necessary articles of worship it may care to obtain.

Samaritan High Priest with Torah scroll believed to be "thousands of years" old, photographed in Shechem.

The members will then elect their officers to handle the work of organizing the synagogue. Unless the members can afford salaried officials, one or more from among them will begin to serve as cantor, *gabbai*, and *shammash*, providing that each one knows how to perform his duties properly. Even though a congregation needs to have the services of a rabbi to act as a spiritual leader, teacher, and guide, his presence is not absolutely necessary for the conducting of prayer services. Any capable layman may do this work, and many small congregations do not have a rabbi.

However, whenever the congregation is ready to hire a rabbi, cantor, and *shammash*, it must take great care to choose the proper person for each position.

In addition to offering prayer services, the synagogue should also be functioning as a *Bet ha-Midrash* and a *Bet ha-Knesset*, as has already been indicated. As the synagogue grows in membership and gains more support, it will be able to offer additional activities. It may also move to larger quarters and engage additional paid workers. The success of the congregation will depend upon many factors, among them the leadership ability of its rabbi, the amount of cooperation received from its members, worshippers and followers, and the service which it offers to its local community.

Torah Ark of Conegliano Veneto, Italy, 17th century.

SOME ADDITIONAL FACTS REGARDING A SYNAGOGUE ORGANIZATION

1) Financial Support

A synagogue is usually supported largely by the dues paid by its members; by donations from members or other individuals; through fund-raising projects such as bazaars, banquets, etc., as well as from many additional sources.

2) Daily Cash Offerings

Because money may not be handled on Sabbaths or festivals, most synagogues usually have a *pushke*, or a metal box in which worshippers may leave their free-will offerings during week days.

3) The Obligations of a Member

By becoming a synagogue member, it is understood that a person is also expected to take upon himself the support of the synagogue to the best of his ability.

4) Rights of Members and Worshippers

Being a member of a congregation does not require being a worshipper of a particular synagogue, nor is a worshipper asked to become a member. However, during the High Holy Days, when seating space is usually scarce in most synagogues, the congregation may only permit members to occupy the main sanctuary. But a place is often provided for non-members or for those who cannot afford to purchase a ticket. In most other instances anyone is free to enter any synagogue during services.

5) Synagogue and Community

Not only does a synagogue exist for its members and worshippers, it also joins in many community activities. Thus, whenever money is raised for the local community as well as for Jews everywhere (including Israel), the synagogue will nearly always join in such a drive. It will likewise work with other local congregatons and other Jewish organziations for the welfare of our people everywhere.

6) Attending Synagogue Services

It is most desirable for you to pray with a congregation, and you should make every effort to do so. If possible, you should even try to be among the first ten worshippers, because, according to our sages, each of the first ten men to attend receives all the combined blessings of those who come afterwards. But above all, it is only in the presence of a *minyan* that the complete service can be recited.

However, if synagogue attendance is not possible for you, you should then pray alone, and strive to do so at the same time that the congregation prays. (Be sure to check the time of services.) This will be one way of showing your feelings of unity with those who are attending.

BEHAVIOR IN A SYNAGOGUE

Inasmuch as a synagogue is a holy place which is to be revered and respected as though it were the Temple itself, there are certain rules and restrictions regarding synagogue behavior which must be observed. It is because the synagogue is called a *mikdash me'at* (small sanctuary) that we must be so watchful of our conduct while present there. Here are a few rules to follow:

1) It is forbidden to eat or drink while in a synagogue.

2) Running about in a synagogue is also not permitted. One must walk with the greatest dignity and respect.

3) It is likewise forbidden to use the synagogue (even an unused one) as a "shortcut," even if no services are in progress. In case it should be necessary to pass through the synagogue to another destination, it is then proper to sit down for a moment or two before proceeding.

4) During services, whispering, conversing, or doing anything else in the nature of a disturbance is strictly forbidden, it being a sign of disrespect.

WHY YOU AND THE SYNAGOGUE NEED EACH OTHER

From what has been said so far in this chapter, let us now see just how you, as a Jew, maintain a mutual relationship with the synagogue. In simpler language, you and the synagogue both need each other in one way or another. You exist for the synagogue and the synagogue exists for you, as the following points will reveal.

1) The Minyan

Quite often you may be thinking to yourself or telling others: "Why do I have to go to the synagogue? I'm just one person. What will it matter if there is one less person there?"

But do you realize that without you the synagogue services cannot even get started? Why not? Because it takes a *minyan* to hold services. And if everyone were to stay away, no *minyan* could take place. So remember, *you* are that tenth man, and it is up to you to enable the services to function.

As far as you are concerned, you cannot fulfill your total duty as a worshipper without a *minyan*. Thus, unless a *minyan* is present, certain prayers (such as the *Kaddish, Borkhu* and others), cannot be recited, nor can the Torah be read. Without a *minyan* everyone would have to pray as an individual and would not be performing his entire obligation, because his prayers would thus remain incomplete.

2) Conducting Services

Just as the Temple during ancient times was the only place where services, as commanded by our Torah, could be held, so today is it only in the synagogue (or wherever a *minyan* is present) that prayer services may be conducted. The synagogue thus serves as the central place where you can expect to find services being performed. However, the synagogue, in turn, is depending upon you to be there so that those services can take place.

3) To Serve as a *Bet Tefillah*, as a *Bet Midrash* and as a *Bet Knesset*

As you have already seen, the work of the synagogue is not complete unless it has provided you with a place for worship, with a House of Study, and with a Community Center. For Jewish life to function properly, the synagogue needs Jews like you so that it can continue to exist in that capacity. You, on the other hand, require these three types of services so that you will be able to live a full Jewish life by praying, studying, and coming together with other Jews.

4) To Show That We Are United Before God

Whenever we pray together with other Jews, we stand united before God. This unity makes our prayers that much more effective.

For this purpose each and every one of us is needed for services. The more the better.

Then, for your part, by being present at services you are doing your duty in strengthening this unity before the Almighty. Praying with a congregation encourages you to feel all the more proud of being a Jewish worshipper.

5) The Synagogue as Your Home

A home without any occupants is merely a house, not a home. That is exactly what a synagogue would be like without worshippers. That is why the synagogue cannot exist without you.

As for yourself, being a Jew, the synagogue is your home (or at least your "second home"), because that is where you belong. It is there that you are made to feel at home with your fellow Jews, as well as with the prayers you recite and the Jewish knowledge you gain there. The synagogue is there for your benefit. It is up to you to make use of it as *your* home.

6) The Synagogue's Contribution to Civilization

It has been said that "no human institution has had a longer continuous history than the synagogue, and none has done more for the uplifting of the human race."

As you may know, both the Christian church and the Moslem mosque owe their existence to the synagogue. Both of them followed the general plan of the synagogue's service, including such things as prayer, reading from their holy writings, sermons, and other rituals. They each adopted this plan primarily because it was found to be best suited to their religious needs, and they have practiced it ever since.

Therefore, inasmuch as the value of our synagogue has been made clear to many other peoples for hundreds of years, how much more should we, as Jews, appreciate the glorious institution which is our synagogue?

Alms box from synagogue in Piotrkov, Poland, 19th century.

7) Jewish Survival

One reason why the Jewish people have survived is that we have followed the ways of our forefathers and our ancestors. The synagogue is one institution that has guided us throughout each succeeding generation. It has survived because our people have felt the need for it and have maintained it.

Today, that same synagogue still needs worshippers who will make use of it and thus enable it to continue to survive. You are one of those many followers upon whose presence the synagogue depends today, so that there will still be a synagogue tomorrow and in the future.

The synagogue gives you the opportunity to do your part in assuring its survival by attending its services and its classes, and by taking part in as many of its activities as you can. The satisfaction you will gain from your participation in the life of your house of worship will be in addition to all the other benefits it can bestow upon you.

I do hope that by now you have come to realize that by working and cooperating with your synagogue, it is you who stands to gain the most from it, rather than the reverse. After all, the Jews were not created for the synagogue; instead, the synagogue came into being for us Jews — including yourself, of course.

And so, it should be obvious to you that if you are a Jew, you need the synagogue.

Ketubah (marriage contract), Reggio Emilia,
Italy, 1776.

MARRIAGE AND DIVORCE IN JUDAISM

MARRIAGE IN JUDAISM

Have you ever attended a Jewish wedding? If so, you have
probably seen that Jewish weddings are both similar to and unlike
those of non-Jews. What is so particularly distinctive about a Jewish
wedding?

First, let us find out what a Jewish wedding ceremony is like. We
shall try to trace it from beginning to end, and we will then talk about
the reasons for many of the customs. After that there will be a discus-

"The Wedding," by Moritz Oppenheim,
Germany, 1961.

sion of what marriage means to a Jew, as well as an account of some of
the benefits of having been married according to Jewish law and living
a married life as a Jew.

I trust that this information will give you a clearer picture of how
a Jewish wedding ceremony and the married life that follows it help a
Jew to enjoy his Judaism.

Since a wedding is so important to the young Jewish couple concerned, it is usually celebrated with great joy and much pomp and
splendor. However, this ceremony must be conducted according to
Jewish tradition. True, many Jewish wedding customs seem to differ
widely in many ways from country to country, but they all are conducted according to the same Jewish law.

It will therefore be the aim of this chapter to make you familiar
not only with some of the most important laws and customs practiced
by Jews but also with their meaning.

78

PREPARING FOR A JEWISH WEDDING

A number of things must be arranged before a Jewish couple can be married. First and foremost, both the bride and groom must be Jewish. That is, they both must have been born of a Jewish mother, because intermarriage (where one of the partners is not Jewish) is strictly forbidden according to Judaism. When one of the partners in a marriage is not Jewish, the attachment of our whole people to Judaism is weakened, and the basis of a Jewish marriage is absent. Such a couple is not likely to keep a Jewish home and raise its children as loyal Jews. This is in addition to the fact that such a couple is not as likely to be as happy together as when both partners are Jewish and share the same beliefs and practices. Of course, where the woman is the one who is not Jewish, the children born of that marriage are also not Jewish.

The question of conversion must always be referred to a competent rabbinic authority on Jewish law.

As soon as the two people decide to get married, they become engaged. The fiancé usually presents his bride-to-be with an engagement ring, which becomes a token of his promise to marry her. However, according to Jewish law, the engagement (or "betrothal") involves much more than merely the gift of a ring. This ceremony will be discussed in more detail later.

It is to be taken for granted that the couple will also have obtained the necessary marriage license from the civil authorities and have undergone any health tests that are required by law.

A civil marriage (that is, one conducted by state or other officials) is not recognized by Jewish law. A valid Jewish marriage is one that conforms only to the requirements of Jewish law.

SETTING THE TIME AND PLACE OF THE WEDDING

The couple and the family of each party decide on the date of the wedding. Weddings can be celebrated on most days in the Jewish calendar, with the following exceptions:

1) On Sabbaths, festivals, and the middle days of Passover and *Sukkot*, because a wedding involves a legal contract, and no business may be done during a Sabbath or a festival.

2) During most of the *Sefirah* period, that is, during the forty-nine days between Passover and *Shavuot*, because these are days of sadness.

3) During the three weeks from the seventeenth of *Tammuz* to the ninth of *Av* (the Fast of *Av*), which are the saddest days of our entire calendar. In addition, weddings are forbidden on the following four minor fast days: the Fast of Gedaliah, the tenth of *Tevet*, the Fast of Esther, and the seventeenth of *Tammuz*.

However, apart from these restrictions, a wedding is permitted any day of the week except Friday night or Saturday before dark.

A wedding is usually held in a synagogue or in the home of the bride or groom, although it is also often held elsewhere, such as at a hotel, a club, or a catering hall. A quiet wedding may take place in the rabbi's study as well.

In Israel and other countries, it is the custom to hold the ceremony out of doors (in this case, the banquet and reception are conducted indoors). One reason for this is that we hope that the couple's children will be as "numerous as the stars in the heavens" — just as God promised Abraham (see Genesis 15:5, 22:17).

THE AUFRUF

On the Sabbath before the wedding, it is the custom for the groom to come to the synagogue and be called for an *aliyah* during the reading of the Torah. He recites the usual Torah blessings and may even read the *Haftorah*. Relatives may also be honored in this ceremony, which is called the *aufruf*, "being called up." Usually, but not always, it takes place in the synagogue of the groom's family.

The *aufruf* may occur on a Monday or Thursday morning as well as on the Sabbath, or at any other service when the Torah is read. A light *Kiddush* usually follows the synagogue service.

OBJECTS REQUIRED FOR THE WEDDING CEREMONY

On the day of the wedding, before the marriage ceremony can begin, the following ritual objects must be prepared:

Huppah (marriage canopy)

This canopy usually consists of a decorated silk or velvet cloth supported by four poles. Quite often it is decorated with flowers and other attractive adornments. The couple must stand under the *Huppah* during the entire wedding ceremony.

Ring

During the ceremony the groom places the wedding ring on the bride's finger. The purpose of this is to show that the groom is giving the ring to his bride as a gift and that, from then on, she belongs to him only. According to our rabbis, he must give her an article of some value, but not necessarily an expensive one.

Wine

As part of the ceremony, the couple drinks twice from a cup of wine as a token of joy.

China cup, Germany, 20th century.

80

Ketubah

This is the marriage contract, which sets out the terms of the agreement between bride and groom. According to this document, the groom agrees to support his wife and to fulfill certain other obligations toward her. The bride, in turn, promises to be a good, faithful wife to her husband.

The *ketubah*, which is read during the wedding ceremony in its original Aramaic and is usually translated into English, must be prepared beforehand and signed by two witnesses.

Minyan

A *minyan* (a group of ten adult males) should be present during the ceremony. If, however, this is not possible, the presence of at least two witnesses is sufficient.

THE WEDDING CEREMONY

This is the customary order of the wedding ceremony:

1) The Processional

To the accompaniment of music, the groom enters, escorted by his parents. The bride then follows, escorted by her parents. Other members of the bridal procession may precede the bride. The bride and groom then stand under the *Huppah*.

2) The Rabbi's Invocation

The rabbi greets the bridal couple, chanting a Hebrew blessing of welcome in which he asks God to bless them. During the ceremony the rabbi also talks briefly to them, explaining the importance of marriage and of establishing a good Jewish home.

Wall decoration, 19th century. Inscription: "Thy wife shall be as a fruitful vine" (Psalms 128:3).

3) The Blessing of Betrothal (over a cup of wine)

The rabbi or cantor next recites two blessings, one over the wine and another in which he thanks God for allowing the couple to be legally married, according to the laws of God and Israel, and under the *Ḥuppah*. The bride and groom then drink from the first cup of wine.

4) The Ring Ceremony

As the groom places the ring on the bride's right index finger, he recites the following words in Hebrew:

Haray at m'kudeshet li b'taba-'at zu k'dat Moshe v'Yisrael.
("Behold you are consecrated unto me with this ring [as my wife], according to the law of Moses and Israel.")

A marriage ceremony in the Rothschild Family, London, 1857.

This ceremony ends the betrothal portion of the wedding, that is, the part where the couple pledge their faith to each other — the groom by giving the bride the ring and by reciting the above words, and the bride by her acceptance of the ring.

5) Reading of the Ketubah

Before the marriage becomes official, the rabbi reads the *ketubah* aloud before all present so that the bride and groom know what their rights and obligations are. This ceremony also helps to divide the betrothal part of the ceremony from the final act of marriage.

6) The Seven Blessings (over the second cup of wine)

The Seven Blessings *(sheva berakhot)* are then chanted by the rabbi or cantor or, sometimes, by guest rabbis, each one reciting one blessing. In these seven blessings we thank God for having created man and for having gladdened the couple through their marriage. The bride and groom then drink from the second cup of wine.

7) Breaking of the Glass

The groom then breaks a glass by stepping on it. This act concludes the marriage ceremony.

The breaking of the glass is meant to remind us that, even in the midst of such a joyous occasion as a wedding, we must never forget that the Temple in Jerusalem was destroyed and that it has not yet been rebuilt. So we try, at least to some extent, to moderate our happiness at this joyous event.

The wedding is followed by the *yihud* ceremony, which will be described later on. Then come the wedding reception and banquet, complete with joyous music, dancing, eating, and drinking, as well as other forms of merrymaking. The seven blessings that were recited during the wedding ceremony are repeated at the wedding feast. This time, it is the custom to have each blessing recited by members or guests of the two families.

SOME ADDITIONAL JEWISH MARRIAGE PRACTICES AND CUSTOMS

There are many unusual customs relating to the marriage ceremony that have developed in different countries where Jews have lived.

The Tenaim Ceremony

Even though the betrothal is a basic part of the wedding ceremony, many Jews have a separate engagement ceremony before the actual wedding. This is called the *tenaim*, or "conditions" or "terms" of the marriage, because at the ceremony a preliminary marriage agreement is drawn up by the parents of the couple. The *tenaim*, or the terms agreed upon, include the date of the wedding, the amount

Marriage rings, Venice, 16th century.

of dowry to be given by the bride, and the gifts that are expected of the groom. All these conditions are written down, and then, after a plate is broken (an act that is similar to the breaking of the glass at the wedding), there is much feasting, dancing, and merrymaking.

Goodies at the Aufruf

When the groom is called to the Torah on the Sabbath before the wedding, it is the custom for women to throw candies, nuts, or fruit at him, which the children scramble to pick up. This custom expresses the hope that the couple will have many children and that their married life will be as sweet as the goodies showered upon them.

The Couple Remain Separated Before the Wedding

It is also the custom for the bride and groom not to see each other for a few days before their wedding, which makes their reunion during the ceremony that much more meaningful. In ancient times, and even later times, a bride and groom might often have never seen each other until the actual wedding ceremony. (Compare the Bible story of the wedding of Jacob and Laban's daughters, Genesis 29:21-30.)

Visiting the Cemetery Before the Wedding

If the bride or groom, God forbid, has lost a parent, it is the custom for that person to visit the grave of the deceased as a sign of respect before the wedding. Then the *El Molei Rahamim* (the memorial prayer) is recited.

If such a visit is not feasible, the bride or groom may instead attend a Monday morning or Thursday morning synagogue service, when the memorial prayer can be recited for him or her.

Fasting on the Wedding Day

Another common custom is for the bride and groom to fast on the day of the wedding until after the ceremony. The reason for this practice is that this is a sort of "Day of Atonement" for the couple, cleansing them from all their sins so that they may begin their married life

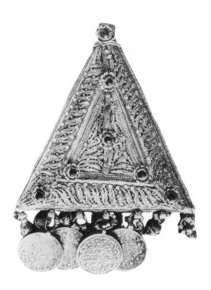

Pendant for a groom, silver with semi-precious stones, Yemen, 19th century.

afresh. However, if the wedding day should fall on *Ḥanukkah, Purim, Lag b'Omer*, the fifteenth of *Av*, or *Rosh Ḥodesh*, it is forbidden to fast, since all these days are either minor festivals or half holidays.

Veiling of the Bride

The special ceremony of the "veiling of the bride" (in Yiddish, *badehken die kalleh*) usually takes place just before the wedding ceremony. The groom, accompanied by the rabbi, the cantor, both sets of parents, and a few relatives, enters the bride's room and covers her face with the veil.

It has been suggested that one possible reason for this custom is to give the groom the opportunity to look at his wife-to-be to make sure that she is the same girl who was promised to him. In this way he would be able to prevent the kind of deception that befell Jacob, who was married to Leah instead of to Rachel (Genesis 29:18-30).

Lighted Candles during the Wedding

Men and women often carry lighted candles in the bridal procession as a sign of light and joy.

Bride Circles Groom

Another custom is one carried out by the bride. As soon as she has entered and before she has stood under the *Ḥuppah*, she walks around the groom three or seven times. Since both seven and three are considered to be numbers of special significance, this may be intended as a guard against evil spirits, to prevent them from entering the circle.

85

Yihud

After the bride and groom have become legally married and the ceremony is over, they enter a private room, where they are alone for the first time as man and wife. For a short while they are allowed complete privacy, or *yihud*. Quite often the newly marrieds break their fast and share their first meal during this period.

A Week of Seven Blessings

The seven blessings are recited not only during the wedding ceremony but also at the banquet, following the "grace after meals." Then, for a whole week following the wedding, the couple presides at festive meals attended by guests, some of whom may have been unable to come to the wedding. Here, too, the seven blessings are recited, special guests or members of the family each being honored with the recitation of one blessing.

Tree Branches for Ḥuppah Poles

In ancient Israel it was the custom to plant a tree when a child was born — a cedar tree for a son and a cypress for a girl. When the children grew up and married, branches from both trees would be used to make the poles of the *Ḥuppah*.*

WHAT MAKES A JEWISH WEDDING JEWISH?

Heartwarming as this Jewish joy is, it is still enjoyed in moderation. Thus, the cries of "mazeltov" as the groom breaks the glass become a reminder that our Temple of old was destroyed. Or, when the bride and groom fast on their wedding day, they realize that their sins are forgiven, so that they can now embark on the sea of matrimony with a clean slate.

Then, when they sign the *Ketubah* and have it read aloud, they thus make it known to all present that they trust each other by agreeing to certain conditions.

The Seven Blessings are an expression of the thanks to God for their having been married according to the laws of Moses and Israel, and to express their joy in the true spirit of our Torah.

*More quaint and unusual customs can be found in the following:
H. Schauss, *The Lifetime of a Jew*, pp. 206-219.
Encyclopedia Judaica, Vol. XI, pp. 1042-1046.
P. and A. Goodman, *The Marriage Anthology*.
L. S. Routhenberg and R. R. Seldin, *The Jewish Wedding Book*, pp. 79-91.

DIVORCE IN JUDAISM

Every couple tries to make their marriage as happy as possible. Sometimes, however, difficulties arise, perhaps because the couple is not really suited to each other. They then should try to settle their differences among themselves.

But, if they have made every effort and their differences are still at the point where they may be doing each other more harm than good by remaining together, there is therefore a need for a Jewish divorce.

The Bible and the Talmud contain certain laws regarding divorce, which is to be performed in a responsible and humane manner.

In fact, it is possibly true that, because Judaism does allow for divorce when necessary, the bond of marriage may be strengthened, since each partner is committed to it purely of his or her own free will, and not because either is under any compulsion.

Really, it is because marriage is so sacred to us that divorce is permitted. A man and woman enter into marriage with the idea that it is a permanent arrangement. However, they also know that it is possible for them to end this arrangement by following the laws of divorce commanded in the Torah and explained by our sages.

They know that they have the choice of breaking off their relationship in a responsible, fair, and humane way, and that they then can remarry if they want to.

Neither of the two is permitted to remarry, however, unless their divorce has been executed according to Jewish law. A civil divorce by itself is not enough.

HOW A JEWISH DIVORCE IS CONDUCTED

Let us now describe what happens in a Jewish divorce. Judaism is one of the few religions that permit a married couple to seek a divorce by mutual consent. Both parties may agree to it of their own free will, without feeling that one or the other is being forced into it in any way.

The actual procedure of the divorce (or, as it is called in Hebrew, the *get*) must be conducted by a *bet din* (Jewish court) consisting of three learned rabbis. In addition to the *bet din*, there must also be a *sofer*, or "scribe," to write the "bill of divorcement" on a scroll of parchment (similar to a Torah scroll, but much smaller) and make out one copy for each party. Two reliable witnesses must also be present.

Of course, before the divorce is granted by the *bet din*, the couple has usually already obtained a divorce through the civil courts, where they settle such matters as money, property, support, and care and custody of children. Even though a civil divorce is necessary under the law of the land, a couple who has gotten only a civil divorce is considered by Jewish law to be still married.

Before the members of the *bet din* order the *get* to be written, they put forth every effort to encourage the couple to change their minds and decide to return to each other. Only if such a reunion is not possible is the *get* drawn up.

The husband must present the *get* personally to his wife, placing it directly in her hands. However, if it is not possible for husband and wife to be in attendance together, the *get* may be delivered to the wife through a *shaliah*, or "messenger."

Unlike the civil bill of divorce, the *get* itself does not contain the grounds of divorce, nor any charges made by one of the partners against the other. It includes only the full names of both parties, the Hebrew and civil dates, and the name of the city and state where the *get* was written, and declares that both the husband and the wife have agreed to this divorce proceeding. There then follow the signatures of the husband and the wife, of the officiating rabbis, and, finally, of the two witnesses.

Following these divorce proceedings, each party is then free to remarry, although there are certain restrictions regarding a remarriage. For example, a divorced woman may not marry a *Kohen* (a person descended from the priestly line), since this is prohibited by Biblical law.

As we study the Jewish laws of divorce, however, let us keep in mind that it is the hope of every Jewish couple to have a happy, lasting, and harmonious marriage.

By trying to live by the Torah, and by following the Jewish way of life, most Jewish couples should be able to live happily together, without any need of divorce. In fact, the rate of divorce among observant Jews is, on the whole, much lower than that among the rest of the population. The aim of the marriage relationship, as the Torah helps to create it, is that it should be a sacred bond of true love.

Hallah cover for the Sabbath and holidays, Germany, 19th century.

KASHRUT: YOU ARE WHAT YOU EAT

INTRODUCTION

You have no doubt heard the word "kosher" used — sometimes even as a slang expression, such as, "It's kosher," meaning "It's OK." You may also know that an observant Jew eats only food that is kosher.

But just what do we mean by "keeping kosher," and why do we do it? Before learning about *kashrut*, which forms an essential part of Jewish life, we must first be sure we understand the terms mentioned thus far.

"*Kosher*" means that which is in accordance with the laws of *kashrut*, the Jewish dietary laws. The dietary laws deal with kosher food, that is, food that is permitted by Jewish law to be eaten.

Incidentally, the word "kosher" itself, as well as referring to the laws of *kashrut*, simply means "fit," "proper," "correct," "permitted," and can also be applied to a Torah scroll, an *etrog* (citron used during the festival of *Sukkot*), a *tallit* (prayer shawl), or *tefillin* (phylacteries used during weekday prayers) — all of which must be kosher, that is, fit for use, from a halakhic (Jewish law) point of view. Also, a synagogue must be kosher, and even an upright and trustworthy person is often spoken of as being a "kosher" individual.

Because food is such an essential part of life and social relationships, the laws of *kashrut* greatly influence our lives. It is therefore not at all surprising that of the 613 commandments contained in the Torah, fifty deal with food and eating habits. This emphasis is continued by our sages, who have also dealt with the same topic at length in the Talmud and in later works.

The subject of *kashrut* is so complex that this chapter will aim only at giving you a bare outline of the principles behind the dietary laws as they affect our everyday lives. Even though the main topic under discussion will deal with food, especially meat, eating habits as well as certain broader aspects of *kashrut* will also be touched upon.

HOW AND WHY DO WE OBSERVE KASHRUT?

While the reasons for many of our laws are clear to us from studying the Torah, the reasons for other laws cannot be fully understood by human beings. Into this second category of laws, called *hukim*, fall the laws of *kashrut*.

In order to deepen our appreciation of the Jewish way of life, our rabbis have tried to analyze these *hukim* and to suggest the reasons behind them, and some of their reasoning will be discussed in this chapter. But it should always be remembered that we observe all the *mitzvot* of the Torah regardless of whether we know the reasons behind them. Jewish law is to be observed because it was given to us by God Almighty, and the best way to understand and appreciate the *mitzvot* is to observe them.

We observe *kashrut* because the Torah commands us to, and therefore in the deep belief that it is for our own ultimate benefit. Just like all the other commandments of the Torah, *kashrut* has been given to us to enrich and improve our lives. How it actually does so may not always be apparent to us. Even the Bible gives us no specific reason, except to state:

> For I am the Lord your God; sanctify yourselves therefore, and be holy; for I am holy; neither shall you defile yourselves with any manner of swarming thing that moves upon the earth.*

An additional factor makes its entrance in a later chapter:
> You shall be holy unto Me, for I the Lord am holy, and I have set you apart from other peoples to be Mine (Leviticus 20:26).

*Leviticus 11:44. See also Exodus 22:30.

90

Fish plate, Germany, 19th century.

Both of these passages are set forth in the context of the laws of *kashrut.* Our rabbis have suggested that:

1) The dietary laws help to develop the divine quality of holiness in the Jewish people.

2) As well as fostering the bond of holiness between God and Israel, observance of the dietary laws automatically separates us from other peoples who do not keep such rules.

Although our history has shown that keeping kosher has always been good for our health, the Bible mentions nothing about these laws having been given for reasons of health and hygiene. Rather, from studying the Torah, our rabbis have suggested that the laws of *kashrut* are based on moral reasons, in order that we may become holy unto God.

But how can food make one holy, rather than just simply healthy? In order to answer that question, let us see how a piece of kosher meat differs from a piece of non-kosher meat by following the stages in which meat becomes kosher and fit for consumption under Jewish law.

1) The meat comes from a "clean," four-legged animal, that is, one that is permitted to be eaten according to Biblical law.

2) The animal is slaughtered in a proper manner by a qualified *shohet* (ritual slaughterer), as commanded by rabbinical law.

3) After the animal has been killed, its carcass is thoroughly examined by the *shohet* for any possible disease, infection, or other defects that make the animal *trafe* (unkosher), and certain forbidden parts of the animal are removed.

91

4) Before being prepared for eating, the meat is soaked in cool water and thoroughly salted and rinsed so that it is completely drained of all blood.

5) The meat is prepared only in kosher utensils.

6) The meat is kept free from contact with anything else that might render it unkosher, such as dairy foods, non-kosher ingredients, non-kosher meat, etc.

7) The entire system of *kashrut* is under strict supervision by the Jewish community, both in the slaughterhouse and in the meat market, in order to guarantee the right of the Jew to eat kosher meat.

Throughout the whole of Jewish history, experience has shown that observing all these stages of *kashrut* has enhanced the moral and physical well-being of the Jew.

And now to explain each of these more at length and to tell you how they are observed:

1) *For meat to be considered kosher, it first must come only from a four-legged animal that the Bible permits us to eat.*

The Torah permits us to eat only those four-legged animals that have a split hoof *and* that chew the cud (Leviticus, Ch. 11). Note that *both* these conditions must be met before an animal can be considered kosher.*

Most forbidden animals tend to be wild or meat-eating, whereas the permitted animals tend to be herbivorous (living on vegetation) and domesticated. In other words, we Jews are not permitted to eat an animal that preys on other animals.

It has been pointed out that animals who chew their cud generally have longer intestines than meat-eating animals and therefore spend more time in the passive process of digesting their food. On the other hand, it is believed that the shorter intestines of the meat-eaters enable the food to become quickly transferred into the blood, the carrier of the animal instinct. It is likewise believed that, while an animal with an undivided hoof is likely to use his foot as a weapon, those whose hooves are split will use their feet only to stand on.

By observing the laws of *kashrut*, we avoid eating animals that display these savage habits. It is thought that we thus become more humane and considerate of other human beings as well as of animals.

A further restriction is that only an animal which is entirely healthy and free from defects is a fitting object for ritual slaughter.

2) *For the meat of a permitted animal to be considered kosher, it must be slaughtered only according to rabbinical law and by a qualified shohet.*

The laws of *shehitah* (ritual slaughter) are very detailed and must be carried out by a qualified *shohet*. The *shohet* must be not only an

---

*Although we do not observe *kashrut* for health reasons, it is still nice to know that keeping kosher has kept Jews free of diseases such as trichinosis, which comes from pig meat, and tularemia, which comes from rabbit meat.

expert at what he is doing but also a strictly observant Jew who follows the laws of *Shabbat, kashrut,* and all other *mitzvot* of the Torah. While the butcher of non-kosher meat is an ordinary person who kills the animal in any way that serves his purpose, the *shohet,* in addition to being a highly skilled expert in his work, must be a scholar and an individual of unquestionable high moral character. From this alone you can judge the great stress that Judaism places upon the need to treat animals considerately and humanely.

The detailed laws of slaughtering animals and fowls are considered to cause the animal a minimum amount of pain and to kill it instantaneously. The *shohet* must be well learned in these laws. Furthermore, he must also possess an exact knowledge of the anatomy, organs, and diseases of the animals he slaughters, and must be fully competent in the proper Jewish method of slaughtering animals. The *shohet's halef* (slaughtering knife) must always be kept sharp and without any nicks or other defects, thereby causing as little pain to the animal as possible.

It is felt that if, in fact, life must be taken, let it at least be done in the most humane manner possible. Even an animal should not be allowed to suffer needlessly. Thus, the person entrusted with the sacred task of slaughtering an animal according to rabbinical law must always keep in mind the seriousness of what he is doing when he inflicts the fatal blow. This procedure helps us to see that, as Jews, we have a high regard not only for human life but also for the life of an animal.*

From what has been said, we can appreciate that hunting animals for food is forbidden by Jewish law and that killing for sport (and not for food) would violate Jewish precepts of kindness to animals and of regard for life. The connection between *kashrut* and human behavior has also been suggested by non-Jews. A famous French writer once said that because "no Jewish mother ever killed a chicken with her own hands," murder is so "rare among Jews."

The correct mode of killing an animal, however, is only one stage in guaranteeing the *kashrut* of the meat.

3) *The animal's carcass must be thoroughly examined by the shohet for any possible disease, infection, injury, or any other defect which makes the animal trafe. Also, certain forbidden parts of the animal must be removed.*

The sages of the Talmud have laid down many detailed indications to determine whether a properly slaughtered animal or fowl is kosher or *trafe,* that is, whether it is fit, or unfit, for eating. Although, as stated earlier, we do not observe the laws of *kashrut* for health reasons, the fact that slaughtered animals require examination indicates that *kashrut* observance makes good health sense. In other words, whereas, among non-Jews the inspection of meat is left to the civil authorities, Judaism makes this practice a required part of our religion.

*For further details regarding Shehitah, see S. Freedman, *The Book of Kashruth,* J. Cohn, *The Royal Table,* and Dayan I. Grunfeld, *The Jewish Dietary Laws,* Vol. I.

Kosher Cuts of Beef

Kosher Cuts   Non-Permissible Cuts

Also, before the meat may be sold, veins and blood vessels and certain tendons must be removed by the butcher. Other forbidden portions of the animal which must also be removed include the fat portions (called *helev*) that are attached to the stomach and the intestines, as well as certain other fat parts.

These are some of the duties of a *shohet*. Should any doubts of any kind arise, he will usually consult another *shohet*, or a rabbi.

Many highly observant Jews will not eat meat unless it is *glatt kosher*, a term referring to the lung of the animal being perfectly smooth (*glatt*, in Yiddish) and entirely free of scabs. If the lung does contain scabs that have been perfectly healed, the meat is still acceptable to most rabbinical authorities. Nevertheless, some pious Jews will only eat meat that is *glatt kosher*.

After the meat has passed full inspection, the *shohet's* duty is over. However, meat markets where it is sold must have only kosher food on display and be closed on the Sabbath and festivals, and the meat dealer must be an observant Jew. In this way, we insure that the meat will be properly looked after so that it may remain as kosher as when it left the slaughterhouse.

4) *Before being prepared for food, the meat must be soaked in cool water and then thoroughly salted and rinsed in order to drain it of all blood.*

Meat from the slaughtered animal must be thoroughly drained of blood before we are allowed to eat it. In several different places we find that the Bible strictly prohibits the eating of blood because blood is regarded as the seat of life of an animal. Since blood is the substance that keeps the body alive, drinking blood has been compared to drinking the very life of the animal. So serious is the prohibition against eating blood that even an egg containing a blood spot may not be eaten.

Since the germs of many diseases are carried in the bloodstream, it is hygienic to drain the meat carefully — another health benefit to be gained from keeping kosher — although, again, it is not because of this reason that we keep kosher.

The meat is first soaked in cool (but not very cold) water for half an hour in order to remove the surface blood and open the pores gradually. It is then ready for salting. After being laid out on a special slanted board (so that any additional blood may flow down), the meat is thoroughly sprinkled with heavy salt and allowed to stand for one hour. Following this, the salt is shaken off and the meat is washed again three times in cool water to rinse off all the blood.* Some meats, especially liver, can be "kashered" (made kosher) only by broiling them over an open fire instead of by salting them, since salting will not remove all the blood.**

If the meat has not been kashered (soaked and salted) within seventy-two hours after being slaughtered, it should be soaked or washed in cool water so that the pores will remain open for salting. This must be done either by the butcher or by the housewife.

5) *The meat must be stored, prepared, and served only in kosher utensils.*

Kosher utensils, including cutlery, dishes, pots, pans, appliances, stove, oven, refrigerator, sink, etc., are those that have never come in contact with non-kosher substances or that have been made kosher according to Jewish law.

But keeping kosher also requires a total separation between meat and milk. Thus, in a kosher kitchen milk and meat utensils are kept separate, in accordance with the Biblical command, "You shall not boil a kid in its mother's milk" (Exodus 23:19). The Bible gives us no reason for this separation, but it does tell us in the same context that we are a "holy people unto the Lord" (Deuteronomy 14:21).

Although we keep *kashrut* because it is God's will that we should, we know that He made these rules for our own ultimate good. Scholars have pointed to the fact that the prohibition against mixing milk and meat agrees with our deepest ethical feelings. When we are about to benefit from the fact that a fellow creature has been deprived of life, we should at least not show ourselves so heartless as to cook it in the milk of the animal who might have given it life, that is, to "boil a kid in its mother's milk."

Some scientists believe that the unequal rate of digestion of meat

---

*When purchasing kosher meat, one should find out whether it has already been properly kashered.
**See I. Grunfeld, *The Jewish Dietary Laws*, Vol. I, pp. 103-110.

and milk foods may be one reason why eating them together is prohibited. Also, Moses Maimonides, the famous scholar and physician of the twelfth century, believed that the combination of meat and milk may have a harmful effect on the body.

The prohibition against mixing milk and meat includes not only all meat and dairy foods but also everything with which they may come into contact. That is why kosher households contain different dishes, utensils, pots, and pans for both milk and meat. It is usually best to use utensils of a different color or design for milk and meat, and to keep them in a separate place. Cutlery and linen should also be differentiated. If meat and dairy foods are being cooked on the same stove, special care should be taken to prevent their being mixed.

6) *The meat must be kept strictly separate from any contact with anything that may make it unkosher.*

Even though all the above-mentioned steps have been faithfully followed, if the meat should come into contact with anything *trafe* at any stage, it immediately becomes *trafe*. From this you can appreciate that for *kashrut* to be kept properly, it must be kept completely.

Therefore, the *kashrut* of any foods used together with meat also needs to be checked to see if these foods contain any non-kosher or dairy ingredients. A competent rabbinical authority should be consulted whenever a question arises as to the *kashrut* of a product.

After eating meat, you must wait from three to six hours before eating any dairy food, to allow time for digestion. (There is a difference of opinion as to the exact interval, depending upon the custom you follow.) Meat may usually be eaten after dairy foods (except in the case of some hard cheeses, which take a long time to digest); however, you should first rinse your mouth with water before eating the meat.

7) *In every Jewish community where kashrut is observed, there is an organization that insures that the laws of kashrut are being fully observed.*

The *Va'ad ha-Kashrut* (Kashrut Committee) is held responsible for enforcing every aspect of *kashrut*, from the slaughterhouse until the meat reaches your home.

This *Va'ad* appoints a *mashgiah*, or inspector, who is familiar with all the laws of *kashrut*, to supervise the *kashrut* of the *shohet*, the slaughterhouse, and the meat market.

The duties of the *mashgiah* include insuring that the *shohet's halef* is always sharp, that the slaughtered animal has been properly examined, and that the packing plant keeps its facilities in suitable order for the slaughtering, examination, and packing processes. He must also make certain that no non-kosher meat is brought in or shipped out to be used as kosher meat. As soon as an animal has been properly slaughtered and has passed inspection, it is stamped with a "kosher" label.

Apart from his duties in the slaughterhouse, the *mashgiah* usually also supervises the markets, checking to see that only kosher meat is

Milk and meat areas as they are separated in the kitchen.

sold there, that the Sabbath and festivals are being observed by the butcher, and that meat is not kept for seventy-two hours without first being properly soaked with cool water — all this in addition to any other matters relating to the full observance of *kashrut*.

In this way you are assured that the meat that comes to your table has gone through the correct preliminary processes that guarantee perfect *kashrut*.

OTHER PERMITTED AND FORBIDDEN FOODS

What Makes Them Kosher or Trafe?

The laws of *kashrut* deal not only with the meat of quadrupeds (four-legged animals), but there are also laws governing the eating of other foods, such as fowls, fish, milk, and dairy products, as well as fruits and vegetables.

A. Poultry and Fowls

Since most of the seven steps that we have seen regarding quadrupeds generally apply to fowls as well, this section will deal only with certain differences in the laws of *kashrut* as they apply to fowls.

1) Permitted and forbidden fowls

The Bible does not lay down any specific rules for identifying fowls as it does for quadrupeds. It only tells us: "Of all clean birds you may eat" (Deuteronomy 14:11) and then goes on to list twenty-four types of forbidden birds without stating what exactly is meant by a "clean bird." (Compare Genesis 8:20, where Noah offered a "clean fowl" as a thanks offering to God after leaving the Ark.)

Just as a quadruped's eating habits are often associated with its being "clean" or "unclean," so birds of prey are forbidden as food. It is thought that the person eating the flesh of a bird with such cruel habits may be similarly affected. The eggs of any unclean fowl are also forbidden to be eaten.

For a bird to be permitted to be eaten, it must have a projecting claw, a crop, and a gizzard or stomach that can readily be peeled off its inner lining. Since there is some difficulty in determining which birds are kosher, today we eat only those that have always been traditionally acceptable, such as chickens, ducks, geese, turkeys, and doves.

The eggs of non-kosher birds can usually be identified by their shape — they are usually round instead of oval. Also, unlike that of clean birds, the yolk is usually outside the white.

Still another indication of a wild (and, therefore, forbidden) bird is that it will snatch pieces of food directly from the air, instead of first placing them on the ground before eating them, as a clean bird will do.

2) Slaughtering

The basic principles of slaughtering a fowl are primarily the same as those for quadrupeds.

Following the slaughtering of a fowl, its blood must be covered with sand or soil, after having fallen on other sand or soil previously spread out on the floor. This act is based on a Biblical commandment that the rabbis have interpreted to refer to both birds and wild beasts, but not to domestic animals. (See Numbers 19:17 and Leviticus 17:13.)

3) Examination of the slaughtered bird

In the past, the examination following the slaughtering of a fowl was usually made, not by the shohet, but by the housewife. However, most poultry today is examined in the meat market or, if it is frozen, in the packing plant. The butcher who examines the fowls must, like a shohet, be a fully trustworthy and observant Jew.*

4) Draining of the blood

Here, the same rules apply as for other animals. In removing the feathers of the fowl, care should be taken not to dip the fowl in hot water, as it is strictly forbidden to dip any animal or fowl in hot water before being kashered. The hot water can interfere with the proper draining of the blood and can create other problems as well.

5) and 6) Separation from anything likely to make it trafe

The same precautions are to be followed as those for other meat.

7) Supervision of kashrut

Most supervision of poultry is done at the kosher meat market, under a qualified mashgiah, just as it is for other meat. To every slaughtered fowl a plumba (special lead tag) is attached, indicating that it has been properly slaughtered.

Although the kashering of a fowl is slightly simpler than that of a quadruped, it rightly falls into the same seven stages, which must be adhered to carefully. Only the bare outlines of the laws of kashrut for both fowls and animals have been presented here. For a more detailed account of these laws, the reader is referred to the section entitled "For Further Reading."

B. Fish

For a fish to be kosher it must have both fins and scales, not only one or the other. This law would therefore rule out such creatures as shellfish, lobsters, oysters, clams, and shrimps.

Not only are these sea animals trafe according to Jewish law, they are also considered to be unhealthy and sources of disease since they usually live in infected waters.

A fish that has scales generally has fins as well, but that does not necessarily mean that a fish with fins also has scales. Each such fish must be examined separately.

---

*J. Cohn, The Royal Table, pp. 67-72.
No one may examine a fowl without first being thoroughly trained in this procedure.

Even if the scales of a fish fall off after leaving the water, it may still be eaten, but if the fish's scales fall off while still in the water, it is *trafe*.

Some examples of kosher fish are pike, trout, salmon, carp, halibut, and sole. Lists of kosher fish may be obtained from the UOJCA, 116 East 27th Street, New York, New York 10016.

The laws of slaughtering do not apply to fish, according to Numbers 11:22, wherein we are told, "If flocks and herds *be slain* for them . . . or if all the fish of the sea *be gathered together* for them . . ."

Fish should be thoroughly cleaned before being prepared to be eaten, and utensils that are used to clean, cut, and weigh, as well as to cook and serve the fish, must all be kosher.

C. Milk and Dairy Products

Products such as these are usually considered to be kosher as long as they contain no unkosher ingredients and the milk does not come from a non-kosher animal.

In order to avoid the possibility that cow's milk may be mixed with that of a horse, a pig, or any other non-kosher animal, many observant Jews today will use only *halav Yisrael*, milk produced by an observant Jew. On the other hand, many other Jews rely on strict U.S. Government inspection of milk, which prohibits such a mixture, and therefore will drink Government-inspected cow's milk even if it has been produced by non-Jews.

Even though milk as it is now produced in the United States is hardly likely to come from unclean animals, there still remains a risk that certain kinds of milk may contain ingredients like mono- and di-glycerides, many of which do come from the inner organs of animals. Also, cheeses often contain ingredients such as rennet, which comes from the stomach of a calf. Only cheeses produced under rabbincal supervision may be eaten.

D. Fruits and Vegetables

All fruits and vegetables are usually kosher. However, a few vegetables are forbidden to be eaten on Passover. Also, *orlah* — fruit from a tree less than three years old — may not be eaten (Leviticus 19:23-25).*

E. Other Foods

Any processed foods or drinks may contain non-kosher ingredients. Therefore, the *kashrut* of all processed foods should be checked. These include breads, pastries, candy, gum, canned and frozen foods,and any other processed foods.**

*For additional restrictions on agricultural products, see I. Grunfeld, *The Jewish Dietary Laws*, Vol. II, pp. 34-40; J. Cohn, *The Royal Table*, pp. 111-123.
**Of great help to the kosher consumer are certain rabbinical organizations which supervise many nationally distributed products and show their endorsement by a symbol on the label.
In addition, wine requires kosher supervision.

HOW A QUADRUPED BECOMES KOSHER IN SEVEN STEPS

(Based on General Description and Discussion in Text)

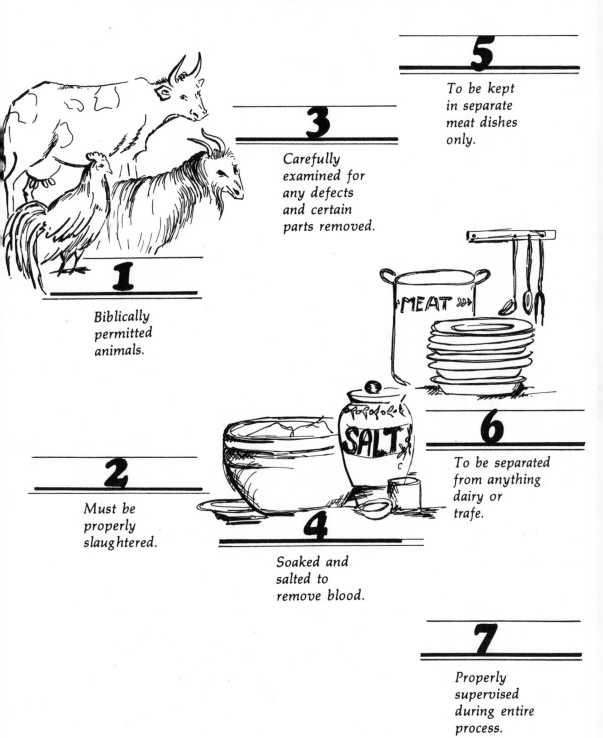

5
To be kept
in separate
meat dishes
only.

3
Carefully
examined for
any defects
and certain
parts removed.

1
Biblically
permitted
animals.

6
To be separated
from anything
dairy or
trafe.

2
Must be
properly
slaughtered.

4
Soaked and
salted to
remove blood.

7
Properly
supervised
during entire
process.

If the observance of *kashrut* requires so much care throughout the year, it is even more exacting on Passover.

Before you buy any food to be used for Passover, you must always look for the label "kosher *l'Pesaḥ,*" which means that a particular product may be used for Passover. This information must be part of the label of a reliable company recognized for its proper standards of *kashrut* for Passover, or must be accompanied on the label by a signed certification of a competent rabbinical authority.

If a product does not have this special label, it may well contain *ḥametz.* Just as the opposite of "kosher" is *trafe,* so the opposite of "kosher *l'Pesaḥ*" is *ḥametz.* The term *ḥametz* actually means "leaven," and derives from the story of the departure of the Israelites from Egypt. At that time the bread they had begun preparing did not have a chance to leaven and rise. The dough fell flat and became *matzo.* For this reason, as a reminder of the haste with which our forefathers had to leave Egypt, and as a sign of the freedom they won, they were commanded by God not only to eat *matzo* instead of bread but also not to eat any food containing *ḥametz.* Since this is one way of remembering and observing this festival, Passover is also called *Ḥag ha-Matzot,* or the Festival of Unleavened Bread.

In fact, eating *ḥametz* on Passover is considered even more serious an offense than eating anything *trafe,* as we find in the following verse from the Torah:

> "Seven days shall there be no leaven found in your houses; for, whosoever eateth that which is leavened, that soul shall be cut off from the congregation of Israel, whether he be a stranger, or one that is born in the land." (Exodus 12:19; see also Exodus 12:15.)

As an example of this difference between *ḥametz* and *trafe,* consider that if a drop of milk falls into a meat dish more than sixty times its volume, it may not always make that meat *trafe.* On the other hand, *any* amount of *ḥametz,* no matter how small, is enough to disqualify any Passover food with which it comes into contact and to make it entirely forbidden.

Due to space limitations, the actual laws of *kashrut* for Passover cannot be discussed in this volume, and the reader is referred to Dayan I. Grunfeld, *The Jewish Dietary Laws,* Vol. I, Chapter 16, for a discussion of these laws.

Here is something to keep in mind for after Passover. *Ḥametz* owned by a Jew or by an establishment owned by a Jew during Passover is forbidden ever to be eaten by Jews. Therefore, in order to be sure that after Passover you are not violating this law, at the close of the festival it is best to wait for a certain period of time before buying food from stores under Jewish ownership and before eating *ḥametz* in the home, restaurant, or other establishments of a Jew, unless, of course, you know that the owners properly sold all of their *ḥametz* before Passover. The length of time necessary to wait before obtaining food from Jews after Passover may vary from place to place, according to how long it takes to exhaust the supply on hand. In the case of stores, many Jews wait several weeks; however, it is best to consult a rabbinical authority if in doubt as to the proper amount of time to wait. Ḥametz that was owned by a non-Jew during Passover may be purchased after the holiday providing you are certain that the food he sells is kosher.

ADDITIONAL ADVANTAGES TO
KEEPING KOSHER

By eating only the kinds of foods that our Torah permits and not just anything we may like, we have the opportunity to set ourselves apart from the animal world and to develop certain habits of discipline and self-control. These habits can aid us in so many areas of our lives,

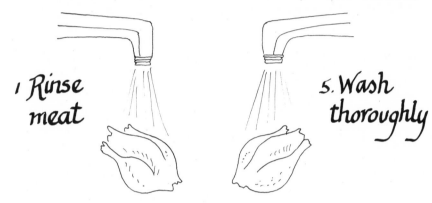

1 Rinse meat

5. Wash thoroughly

How to Kosher Meat

2. Soak in water for half hour

4. Salt and let sit for one hour

3. Drain

whether in our studies, in our profession, or in dealing with other people. The habit of self-control may also help to explain why murder and other violent crimes are usually so rare among Jews.

Alcoholism has likewise never been a problem among observant Jews, despite the fact that, as Jews, we have constant contact with liquor, whether it is for *Kiddush* on *Shabbat* and festivals or for social occasions when we drink a *l'hayyim*. On Purim we are even encouraged to get a bit drunk! Nevertheless, the self-discipline of the Jew may easily explain his freedom from problems of alcoholism.

Furthermore, when you keep kosher you feel that much closer to your fellow Jews, wherever you may meet, who also observe the laws of *kashrut.* You are brought together in a common bond of observance of the ways of the Torah.

Eating kosher also makes you a more loyal Jew as you thus show greater respect for our Torah. Remember, if you are truly sincere about observing *kashrut*, you are doing it not simply because you love to do it or because it is something that sounds reasonable and logical, but primarily because our Torah commands it and because you have full faith in its teachings.

If you have ever felt somewhat hesitant or even embarrassed to eat only kosher food in the presence of non-observant Jews or non-Jews, you have no reason to feel that way. On the contrary, people generally have an inner respect and admiration for those who display honesty and sincerity. They realize that you are being true to yourself and that you are, therefore, someone who can be trusted to be true to others as well.

As for the fear of being different from others by keeping kosher, this is exactly what *kashrut* is meant for. The Bible distinctly commands us to set ourselves apart from non-Jews and their habits of living and to choose the ways of the Torah so that we may become holy unto the Lord (Leviticus 20:26). By setting ourselves apart from non-Jews and following in the ways of the Torah, we show to others a way of life that is worthy of their respect, and thereby serve as a shining example that they may follow. (In fact, many non-Jews observe *kashrut* because of the value they see in it.)

Observing *kashrut* can also lead you to develop more wholesome eating habits. Again, let us review the eating habits of an animal, especially a wild one. In the first place, he generally eats all alone in order to prevent losing any of his food to another animal. As he eats, he keeps one eye on his food, while the other eye guards against anyone who might be coming to snatch that food away from him — in which case he will fight off the intruder to the bitter end.

Compare this with the form of human behavior that a Jew practices when he observes the laws of Judaism. Before anything else, his food must be kosher, as we have already stated. The Jew looks upon his food as something holy and sacred because it is God-given. For this very reason his table is as holy to him as an altar used to be to our forefathers during Temple days.

Therefore, before sitting down to that table, he washes his hands as commanded and then recites a blessing, first over the washing of the hands and then over his bread — the first food that he tastes. Following the meal, he recites the Grace After Meals prayer, thanking God for having given him his food.

Finally, in studying and practicing the laws of *kashrut*, we are reminded of the phrase "You are what you eat." That is, what you eat — and what you do not eat — can have an effect on the type of person you become.

"WHERE THERE IS A WILL, THERE IS A WAY"

If you have now determined to follow the laws of *kashrut*, here is a suggestion to start you on your way. Try to associate as much as possible with friends who also keep kosher. In this way you will not only find it more encouraging to observe *kashrut* yourself, but you will also be helping your friends to do the same.

Today there are more and more kosher products on the market than ever before. Look for them when you shop. They can usually be identified by a special label, such as the Ⓤ symbol, which means that the product has been approved by the Union of Orthodox Jewish Congregations of America.

If you enjoy eating out, you will be pleased to know that there are numerous kosher restaurants throughout the country, located mostly in the larger cities. Several of them even boast Chinese, French or other foreign cuisines. There are also kosher hotels, located mainly in the New York and Miami Beach areas.

Frozen kosher meals are available if ordered in advance on most airlines and on some cruise ships. Many hospitals also keep a supply of these frozen meals.

Unfortunately, not all products that bear the "kosher" label can be trusted to be just that. This is especially true for Passover products, even though they are marked "kosher *l'Pesah*" or "kosher for Passover." The most important way of determining the *kashrut* of any product is to find out whether the rabbi or organization which has approved its *kashrut* is reliable.

Also, any meat market, bakery, hotel, restaurant, or any other business place that sells or serves kosher food should be investigated to see whether its supervision can be trusted.

From what has been written, it is clear that *kashrut* is much easier to observe today than it has ever been before. Kosher food is available no matter where you are, whether in a large city (where it can be easily purchased) or in a small town or even in some out-of-the-way place (where it can usually be brought in). Therefore, for anyone who has the will to observe *kashrut*, the way is wide open and clear.

THE "IS IT KOSHER?" HABIT

Another way of helping yourself along the road to *kashrut* is to develop the habit of always asking yourself, before eating anything of doubtful *kashrut*, "Is this kosher?"

By establishing such a wholesome habit, you will always be on guard against eating anything that may be *trafe*. Then, after this habit becomes firmly fixed within you, as an inseparable part of your life, you will soon find yourself asking the same question, "Is it kosher?" meaning, "Is it proper?" or "Is it right?" when considering any questionable action in your daily life.

Since crimes and other undesirable behavior are often committed in anger or haste, the "Is it kosher?" habit will thus become a most reliable safeguard for you against doing something you may later regret.

In closing, here is a short slogan to guide you as you observe *kashrut:*

"If you keep kosher, *kashrut* will keep you kosher!" Otherwise expressed, this slogan means that if "you are what you eat," your daily conduct will be as kosher as your food.

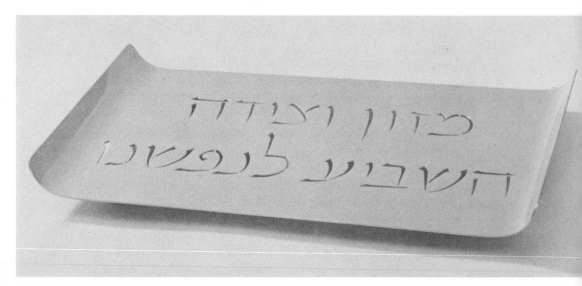

Ḥalla plate, designed by Ludwig Y. Wolpert.

Sabbath candlesticks, silver, Western Europe, late 18th century.

THE HOME IN JEWISH LIFE

Although the Jew has for centuries been surrounded by bitter enemies who sought to destroy him, he has always found renewed strength in his home. He has found his real safeguard, not in physical force, but in his noble way of life. How, then, has it been possible for the Jewish home to remain so strong and to become a living example for other peoples?

In this chapter, we shall examine what Jewish home life is really like and how it has developed. From this we will gain a clearer understanding of what the strength of the Jewish home has always consisted and how we today can help build a healthy family life of our own.

107

It is worthwhile to remember that almost everything in Jewish life has its origin in the home. This is one reason why we Jews have always valued our home life so deeply, and why our survival has been sustained.

It is also worth remembering that nowhere in the Torah or in the Oral Law is it laid down how a Jewish home should be run. All that is demanded of us is that we live by the laws of our Torah. Exactly how we are to apply these basic principles is left entirely to our own good sense, which we are expected to use so that we may do God's will and also live a happy, fruitful, and enjoyable life.

WHAT MAKES A JEWISH HOME JEWISH?

From the outside, a Jewish home looks no different from any other. The first sign of Jewishness is the *mezuzah* on the right doorpost. After you enter, many more things will tell you in what kind of place you are.

But first, let us learn about an old Jewish custom of how a house becomes dedicated as a new home — a custom that even today is still widely observed by a newly-married couple or by people moving into their own place. The ceremony is called *Ḥanukat ha-Bayit*, or "housewarming," and begins by attaching a *mezuzah* to the right doorpost and reciting the following blessing: "Blessed art Thou, our God, King of the universe, who has made us holy with His commandments and commanded us to fasten the *mezuzah*."

Next, certain prayers and Psalms are read, followed by refreshments, singing, and socializing. A scholar may give a lecture on the meaning of this occasion. It is also the custom for relatives and friends to bring bread and salt to the new home, to symbolize good luck.

Now, to return to those things with which the home surrounds itself, giving it its Jewish flavor.

The *mezuzah* on the door, as already mentioned, is there, first of all, because of the Biblical commandment, and also to show that this is a Jewish home. So, whenever you are in a strange neighborhood or in a foreign country and see a *mezuzah* on a door, it is a sure sign that Jews are living there. In fact, there should be a *mezuzah* for nearly every room of the house. (Some additional laws regarding the *mezuzah* are given at the end of this chapter.)

Once inside, your attention will be drawn to the pictures and art objects in the home; you may see a Jewish painting or a figurine made in Israel. Above all, you will never find a typical Jewish home without its books. Apart from the *Ḥumash*, the *Siddur*, the *Maḥzor*, and the *Haggadah*, your attention may be caught by a set of volumes of the Talmud or by other commentaries. There may also be a Jewish encyclopedia and other Jewish reference works. Books on Jewish subjects, either in Hebrew, Yiddish, or English, and special books for children may also contribute to the home's Jewish library.

Jewish newspapers and magazines, too, will be seen around the

Mezuzah wooden holder
containing parchment
manuscript, Galicia, ca. 1850.

Mezuzah case, silver,
Poland, 19th century.

house. It is little wonder, then, that we Jews are known as the "People of the Book"! A Jew feels at home only with his books.

Religious objects are also conspicuous in a Jewish home. Silver candlesticks and *Menorahs* for the *Shabbat* and for *Ḥanukkah*, a spice box, an *ethrog* holder, and possibly a *Purim Megillah* are all there, to be used for each special occasion. Elsewhere, we are sure to see a set of *tallit* and *tefillin*, as well as a specially embroidered cover for *ḥallah* or *matzah*.

Then, in the kitchen, you will find two sets of dishes, one for dairy and one for meat. In addition to these, another such double set will be stored away, to be used for only Passover. As has already been mentioned, only kosher food will be found in a Jewish home.

It takes more than material objects, however, to make a home genuinely Jewish. The family life and relationships must also be conducted according to the laws of the Torah and Jewish tradition.

Since the finest qualities of Jewish family life have developed out of the age-old experiences of our people, it will be helpful to try to discover just how the Jew came to possess those qualities. A glance into our past will supply many of the answers.

THE JEWISH HOME IN THE PAST

If we go back to some of the earliest records of the family in world history, we will find that the family during ancient times differed greatly from the family of today.

For one thing, in addition to the parents and the unmarried children, the ancient family included the married children and their sons and daughters as well. The head of the household, called a "patriarch," usually wielded complete authority. Among some of the Roman and other ancient peoples, the patriarch even had powers of life and death over all those living with him. Among our Jewish ancestors, however, this was not the case.

From our early Biblical history we can learn much about Jewish family life. In the case of the patriarchs mentioned in the Book of Genesis (Abraham, Isaac, and Jacob), we find that the different members of the family showed a great deal of love and respect for one another, even more than in the case of other peoples. This also held true for later generations.

The fifth of the Ten Commandments (Honor your father and mother), which had been observed among the Israelites long before the time of Moses, has continued to be the basis of every Jewish home. Note the wording of this commandment, which says that we should "honor," not "obey," our parents. This means that we should really feel a basic love and respect for them, and not just be obedient.

A beautiful example of the extent of such love and respect may be found in a medieval custom still practiced by some Jews today. When a father or grandfather was called to the Torah for an *aliyah* in the synagogue, his children would get up and remain standing until he returned to his place.*

It was in the home that festivals and celebrations took place, since only a few families could make the pilgrimage to Jerusalem on *Pesah*, *Shavuot*, and *Sukkot*. The festivals, then, became an occasion for family gatherings.

Jewish education also originated in the home. It was once the father's duty to teach his child not only Torah (Deuteronomy 6:7) but also some trade or occupation for earning his future livelihood. The child learned almost everything either from his parents or from brothers, sisters, or other members of the family.

*See Israel Abrahams, *Jewish Life in the Middle Ages*, pp. 122 ff., for additional customs regarding parents and children.

Jewish family celebrating Passover, engraving by B. Picart, 1925.

Even after the Jews had left their land and begun to live among non-Jews, these same Jewish family traditions, which were still observed, served to strengthen their family life, especially when compared to that of their non-Jewish neighbors. In fact, this was so true that the home life of the Jew became a model for other peoples.

Inside the Jew's home there was peace, love, and contentment. Above all, it was the place where he could observe the Sabbath and festivals, study the Torah and teach it to his children, eat and drink as the Torah commands us, and see his children grow up to become proud and devoted Jews.

SOME ADDITIONAL QUALITIES OF JEWISH HOME LIFE

When a Jew went on a journey, a *mezuzah* on a door usually served as his invitation to the hospitality of other Jews. Hospitality became a noted Jewish trait, especially on Sabbaths and festivals.

The Jew's feeling of kindliness was not confined merely to his fellow man. Every living creature had to be treated with kindness and mercy. Jewish law forbids us to cause any creature unnecessary pain or harm. What is more, a Jew is forbidden to sit down to eat before having fed his animals.

When a Jew eats, drinks, or enjoys any pleasure, he does so with a great degree of moderation. The pleasure he derives from acting with moderation is much longer-lasting than that obtained by those who eat or drink to excess.

Also, whenever a Jew washes his hands before a meal, takes a bath before Sabbath or festivals, or rinses his food carefully before eating, he demonstrates a high degree of personal hygiene. This practice has been followed by Jews ever since Biblical days.

There is a familiar saying: "Jews always take care of their own." We Jews are in the habit of practicing *tzedakah*, a term that does not mean "charity," but rather, "righteousness" or "justice." Thus, when a Jew helps his fellowman, he does so not simply out of feelings of pity but because he believes it is his duty to help that person when in need.

Moses Maimonides, the famous medieval philosopher and scholar, has said that the highest level of *tzedakah* is reached when one helps his fellowman to become self-supporting.

A loyal Jew will usually set aside a certain portion of what he earns for *tzedakah*, which can range anywhere from a few coins in the *pushke* (charity box) to the millions of dollars contributed to organizations such as the United Jewish Appeal. The custom of the mother putting a few coins in the *pushke* before lighting her Shabbat candles is one that is typical of how *tzedakah* is practiced and taught in the Jewish home.

A Jew will usually belong to a synagogue and take part in its prayer services and its many other activities. He may also be a member of a Jewish Center or a similar type of organization, and his children will attend a Day school or Hebrew school.

There are many Jewish organizations (such as B'nai Brith, Hadassah, AZA, and Young Israel) to which the various members of the family may belong and the family will try to arrange to live in a Jewish neighborhood for the sake of convenience to the synagogue and to these groups.

Of all the qualities mentioned so far that make a home Jewish, the finest is perhaps *shalom bayit* — good feeling among family members. A Jew tries to win peace not only for his land, but, even more so, for his home. It is only in a home which is at peace that one can live a satisfying Jewish life.

However, if we are to be realistic, we know that, because we are only human, disagreements sometimes arise. Nevertheless, if we really strive for true *shalom bayit*, we are sure to attain our goal.

One way of achieving it is by showing proper respect for the parents as head of the household. They, in turn, should try to earn that respect by their conduct and attitude towards individual members of the family. Honoring one's parents and elders is an almost certain way of establishing *sholom bayit*.

Another possible way to achieve good family relationships is by cherishing the Sabbath and festivals as times when the family can be

Torah pointer, Mediterranean, late 18th century.

together. The Sabbath light is a most reliable symbol of peace leading to *shalom bayit.*

One need not necessarily be rich to have *shalom bayit.* As King Solomon expressed it (Proverbs 15:17): "Far better is a meal of (plain) herbs where love is, than one of a fattened ox when hate comes with it."

Shalom bayit can be present in every home whose members possess a strong enough desire to build toward it.

THE FESTIVALS AND THE JEWISH HOME

A majority of the yearly festivals centers around the Jewish home, which provides a wholesome atmosphere for their observance. Thus, most Sabbath customs are observed in the home. At the beginning of the Sabbath, when the candles are lit by the mother, and continuing through the three Sabbath meals, the Jewish home takes on a special warmth and cheer as the members of the family allow themselves to share their feelings of friendship for one another in a restful atmosphere.

Although much of the High Holy Days is spent in the synagogue, the New Year usually becomes an occasion for family gatherings. Then, on *Erev Yom Kippur,* before the father goes to the synagogue, he blesses his children, just as Jacob did to his children and grandchildren. This custom is also practiced every Friday evening.

On *Sukkot* the family celebrates together and eats a festive meal in the *sukkah. Hanukkah,* of course, is when the family lights the candles, usually with every member participating. The Passover *Seder* also brings the family together to share in the reliving of this glorious holiday.

During all of these festivals and others as well, children usually play an important role, by sharing their joy with other members of the family.

113

THE CHILDREN'S ROLE IN THE FAMILY

The child is often the center of attention in the Jewish family. Following birth, come naming, *Brith Milah* (circumcision), *Pidyon ha-Ben* (redemption of the first-born), Bar Mitzvah, and marriage.

At the same time, the Jewish child must live up to his special duties to his parents. Thus, when parents grow old, it is the child's duty to support them and look after them so that they may continue to live comfortably, happily, and in a dignified way. After the death of a parent, the *Yahrzeit* is observed as a sign of respect. Naming children after deceased relatives allows the survivors to keep their memory alive.

The example that is set by a son or daughter to honor his or her parents will, in turn, most likely be followed by his or her own children during later years.

HOW JEWISH IS YOUR HOME?

Having by now learned something about what a Jewish home was like years ago and what it should be like today, the next question to be determined is whether your home lives up to this standard.

In order to find out the extent of Jewishness in your home, the following steps are suggested:

1) First, review the material discussed in this chapter in order to understand what a Jewish home should be like.
2) Compare this information with the reality present in your home.
3) Decide what to do to improve the situation.

Regarding No. 1, carefully review the foregoing material, including some of the following points: the *mezuzah*, Sabbath and festivals, Jewish books, *kashrut* observance, *shalom bayit*, and *tzedakah*.

For No. 2, you will have to ask yourself whether the objects mentioned in No. 1 that should make your home Jewish are actually to be found there. Then, with regard to No. 3, it will be up to you to decide the following two points:

1) If your home is Jewish in most respects, what can you do to keep it that way, and how can you improve the quality of Jewishness even more? (See below.)
2) If your home is insufficiently Jewish, what can you do to improve the situation? Since this is quite a gigantic task, how can you encourage others in your family to assist you in this effort?

This writer can recall examples in which a single member of a family changed a non-observant home, where practices such as *kashrut* and *Sabbath* were not followed, into an observant one.

Make a list of all the Jewish objects (such as a *mezuzah*, a Hebrew prayerbook, a *Kiddush* cup, and the like) that are lacking in your

Spice container, silver filigree with semi-precious stones and enamel plaques, Italy, 18th century.

home. Then try to obtain those items one by one, through the cooperation of your parents or other members of your family.

Next, follow the same plan with regard to the observance of the Sabbath and festivals, prayer, synagogue attendance, *kashrut*, and whatever else you find to be lacking. Of course, it will first be up to you to set the proper example by observing these practices faithfully. This will be the best way to encourage the other members of your family to do likewise. Also, it is to be understood that you must know something about the meaning of these observances before attempting to convince others to follow them.

Certainly, to undertake the task of converting a non-observant home into an observant one will be far from easy. However, what you will be trying to do is so meaningful that even the slightest measure of success will be well worth striving for.

What is more, if you are really sincere about trying to make your home more Jewish than it is at present, it is very possible that, sooner or later, other members of your family will come to your aid.

The high level of observance you are seeking in your home will eventually add to the good relations of family members because, on the whole, the chances of *shalom bayit* being present in an observant home are far greater than in one that is non-observant.

However, even if you do not succeed in making your family observant, the attempt will eventually reap some benefits for you, as well as for others. First, it will make you become a more loyal Jew, because you will know what your goals are. And, because you know where you are heading, you will gain a greater feeling of self-assurance from the realization that you are doing the right thing. Others, as well as the members of your family, will also come to respect you for your sincerity and for the pride you take in your Judaism.

Above all, as you struggle to make and to keep your home as Jewish as possible, you should constantly be aware of the need to see that others, including your family and friends, also come closer to true, wholesome Jewish living, a state that will become a source of genuine pleasure for them as well as for you.

These are only a few of the advantages to be had by striving to raise the quality of Jewishness in your home.

If, on the other hand, your home is fully Jewish, what should your next step be? The obvious answer is that you should try to keep it that way. For this purpose the following few suggestions may be helpful:

1) If you are a loyal and sincere Jew, you are observing the *mitzvot* primarily because of your deep love and loyalty to the Torah, and regardless of whether you know the reason for their observance. However, you will feel even more confident about your position if you understand the reasons behind the *mitzvot*. In other words, you will find it helpful to know why you are keeping your home Jewish, especially if your position is ever challenged. That is why our sages have warned us: "Know what to reply to a non-believer" (Ethics of the Fathers, 2:19).

In such a case, be sure that you possess enough Jewish learning to be able to defend yourself against an attack by anyone who may challenge matters of observance. If you are not familiar with the reasons for what you do, try to read up on them, or consult a rabbi for advice.

2) Our sages have also warned us: "Make a fence around the Torah" (Ethics, 1:1). By this they meant that, as a rule, you should always be a little stricter in observing a *mitzvah* than you might think necessary. So, for example, in your home you should keep your meat and dairy dishes and utensils in separate cabinets or drawers, to be sure that no confusion occurs.

Another example is the prohibition of handling money on Sabbaths or festivals; this is to insure that you won't use it for buying anything on those days.

So, if you want your Jewish home life to be really strong, you must keep it properly protected by not allowing any of the *mitzvot* to be violated in any way, even seemingly trivial.

3) On the other hand, you should constantly be on the lookout for ways to enrich and beautify the *mitzvot* you do observe in your home.

One way of doing this is to add one or two new books to your Jewish library each year, or more often if possible. Also, you can purchase some Jewish art work, Jewish recordings, and the like. The list of what may be done is endless.

4) If you pride yourself on your high level of Jewish observance, why not invite some of your friends, including those who are not observant, to share these rituals with you? They will most likely welcome the opportunity of seeing sincere Jewish living in action. There is always the

chance that some of them may eventually become influenced by you and follow your example by trying to make their homes as Jewish as yours.

From these few suggestions it should be obvious to you that in a home strongly fortified with wholesome Jewish living, your Judaism will be a source of constant enjoyment and deep pride.

Also, since the home is the birthplace of the Jewish way of life, and of education, religious observance, human conduct, and family relations, it is to be expected that such a place will likewise have an impact on the whole of Jewish society. In other words, a good Jewish home will spread its influence far beyond its immediate confines and will add to the life of the entire Jewish community.

For the achievement of such a goal, anything you can do to make your home Jewish will be most worthwhile.

SOME ADDITIONAL LAWS REGARDING THE MEZUZAH

1) The parchment scroll inside the *mezuzah* case, on which are inscribed two Biblical passages, is what makes the *mezuzah* a holy object.
2) The Biblical passages referring to a *mezuzah* are found in Deuteronomy 6:4-9 and 11:13-21.
3) A *mezuzah* must be attached at each entrance of a house, even if only one of the entrances is used.
4) Each room of the house that is used (except for a bathroom and certain other rooms where it would be disrespectful to place a *mezuah*) requires a *mezuzah*.
5) A house or a room that requires a *mezuzah* must be one that is built for permanent, not temporary, use. A *sukkah*, therefore, does not need one.
6) A *mezuzah* is required for all entrances to a house if they are built with two doorposts and an overhead lintel.
7) Women and children may also attach a *mezuzah*, as long as they understand what they are doing.
8) When moving out of a house, one may leave the *mezuzah* behind if it is known that the next occupant is Jewish. But if the next occupant is a non-Jew, all the *mezuzot* should be removed in order to prevent the possibility of their being treated disrespectfully.
9) The *mezuzah* is never to be thought of as an amulet or a good-luck charm.
10) However, a *mezuzah* without the parchment inside may be worn as a decoration or to identify oneself as a Jew.
11) The *mezuzah* is placed on the right side of a door upon entry.
12) As a sign of respect, it is customary to kiss the *mezuzah* by touching one's fingers to it and then kissing them.
13) The *mezuzah* parchment must be checked every three years to insure that both the letters and the parchment are still intact.

JEWISH PRAYER AND WORSHIP

Did you know that we Jews spend more time in prayer than in any other Jewish activity? We don't set aside one day in the week for prayer, or only one period during the day; we devote ourselves to prayer at least three times in the course of each single day of our lives.

In this chapter I would like to suggest why prayer is so important, and I would also like to touch on how we pray, the contents of the *Siddur*, and other interesting related topics.

WHY DO WE PRAY?

The most obvious reason why we pray is that prayer is one of the 613 commandments of the Torah. In Deuteronomy 11:13, it says, "And you shall serve the Lord your God with all your heart," which our rabbis interpret as referring to prayer. Psalms 100:2 also teaches us to "serve the Lord with joy."

Although both these verses describe the duty of a Jew, it is obvious from the stress on words like "heart" and "joy" that a mere parrot-like recitation of prayers and blessings is not enough. It is only when we come before God with those feelings of honesty, sincerity, and joy as they issue forth from the depths of our hearts that we show our true love for God.

We tell personal things about ourselves only to people to whom we are close, such as parents, relatives, or good friends. But the whole process serves another purpose: in sharing our private thoughts with someone, we feel even closer to that person. So, too, we are drawn closer to God because we express our deepest feelings before Him in prayer.

We want to come closer to God, in the first place, because we know not only that He is the sum total of all goodness, but also that He wants our good and that He is powerful enough to give us everything our heart might wish for and to protect us from evil and unhappiness.

118

Prayer book in silver binding, Italy, 17th century.

But God answers prayer only if it is sincere and "from the heart," and even then He sometimes answers it differently from the way we might expect. The test of true prayer is if we are prepared to accept the answer, whatever it may be, because we pray most of all not to get whatever we want, but to express our love for God.

HOW DO WE PREPARE FOR PRAYER?

Congregational prayer follows a set form and takes place in the synagogue in the presence of a *minyan* at a particular time of day. However, we may make a personal and informal prayer to God at any time or place for something we may very much want: for instance, the recovery of someone we love from a serious illness. On the other hand, we may also offer up a prayer of thanks for some good we have already received, such as having survived a great danger. Thus, the shortest prayer mentioned in the Bible is the one in which Moses implores God to heal his sister Miriam from leprosy. As he was standing before God one day, he suddenly burst out with these five Hebrew words: *Kayl na, refa na lah!* ("O God, please heal her!") There are many more such examples of informal prayer in the Bible, as well as in other Jewish sources.

119

Even though it may seem that the formal type of prayer in which Jews come together for public service is more important, the informal variety is equally meaningful as far as God is concerned. Anyone can pray at any time or in any given place, and as long as his words are sincere, God will listen to him. If this is so, why do we also have to recite prayers at fixed times and in a particular place?

It is certainly true that in Biblical times people used to pray whenever they felt like it. In fact, it would be ideal if everyone could pray naturally and spontaneously, for this is the way prayer should be expressed. However, this is not always possible or practical. Most of us, unhappily, are unable to express ourselves adequately in the language necessary for prayer. We want to use the best words possible to talk to God, and by ourselves we cannot achieve this. Also, few of us are able to organize our thoughts properly enough so that we can say the right things to God at the right time. Furthermore, informal prayer does not tell us when, where, or how to pray, so that our prayers will have some meaning. These are only some of the many reasons why informal prayer is not so ideal after all.

It was because of reasons like these that the Eighteen Blessings, or the *Shemoneh Essrei*, were composed by the members of the Great Synagogue, a group of scholars who dominated the religious life of the Jews who returned to Israel from Babylonia, about twenty-four hundred years ago. The *Shemoneh Essrei*, alternatively known as the *Amidah*, is, in fact, one of the earliest formal prayers that has survived, and so it serves us as a model for the way in which prayer should be expressed.

The requirement that ten adult males (a *minyan)* participate in public worship goes back to Biblical days, when, as we learn in Numbers 14:27, God asked Moses and Aaron, "How long will I have to put up with this evil congregation?" The Hebrew word for "congregation" is *aydah*, and in this case it refers to the Ten Spies who had brought back an unfavorable report about the land of Canaan (Israel). Although this is perhaps the best-known explanation, there are other references in the Torah where the number ten refers to a complete congregation.

A *minyan* is the minimum number of men necessary for the recitation of certain prayers, such as the *Kaddish*, the *Kedushah*, and the repetition of the *Amidah* by the cantor. Public Torah reading may take place only in the presence of a *minyan*.

THE SIDDUR

The Hebrew word for "prayer book" is *Siddur*, which comes from the Hebrew word for "order" and is also related to the word *Seder*, the home service on Passover night. The *Siddur* is so named because it is meant to guide us through the correct order of the prayers. This pattern, as arranged by our sages, corresponds, in general, to the same sequence as the daily sacrifices which were offered in the Temple. As

Hassidic dancing, from a Simhat Torah flag,
Vilna, 19th century.

time passed, other prayers were added, and the whole compilation
became part of our tradition.

The first portion of the *Siddur* is made up of the weekday prayers,
those recited each morning, afternoon, and evening. Then follow the
prayers for the Sabbath and festivals, as well as many other miscellaneous blessings and various portions from the Bible, the Talmud, and
other Jewish literature. Although no two *Siddurim* may be exactly
alike, each adheres to this general arrangement.

Why Do We Need a Siddur for Prayer?

The reason why we need a *Siddur* at all is the same as that given
earlier for formal prayer. Because of our limited knowledge of how to
approach God, we are not able to express ourselves properly if left entirely on our own. By presenting us with a certain number of required
prayers, the *Siddur* gives us something to start off with, while at the
same time allows us to add any private or additional prayers we may
feel necessary to our worship of God.

All over the world, wherever Jews live, they pray according to the
same general order. It is this general uniformity of the *Siddur* that has
done so much to make the Jew feel at home in any synagogue he enters.

The *Siddur*, in addition to helping us pray every day, also gives us
valuable material for study: portions taken from the Bible, the Oral
Law (Talmud), and other Jewish sources. Our most sacred prayer that
we recite three times each day is the *Shema*, taken from the Bible.
Another famous Biblical prayer is the "Song of Moses," which was
chanted after the miracle of the Red Sea.

We say all these Biblical portions every day so that we will always remember to put into practice the valuable lessons they teach us for our daily living. Through constant repetition, the Bible and all the other Holy Writings become alive and meaningful to us every day.

Our prayers generally fall into one or more of the following classes:

1. *Petition:* We ask God to give us something or to do something for us.

2. *Praise and glory:* We praise God in various ways.

3. *Thanksgiving and leave-taking:* We thank Him either for some miracle performed for our ancestors or for some act of kindness done to ourselves. We take leave with words of thanks and gratitude.

The *Amidah* includes all these various kinds of prayer. So, in the first three paragraphs, we praise God for the mighty acts He has performed for the Patriarchs (Abraham, Isaac, and Jacob), for those that He does for us daily, and for being a "holy God."

In the next thirteen paragraphs we ask God to grant our request for such desirable things as intelligence, health, material needs, and the rebuilding of Jerusalem, all of which will help us live full lives as human beings and as Jews. The last three paragraphs contain expressions of thanks as well as of hope for our return to Zion (Israel) and for peace for the Jewish people.

How the Siddur Came About

To appreciate the value of the *Siddur*, we must have some knowledge of how it came into being and how it developed into what it is today.

As mentioned before, the earliest form of Jewish worship was informal prayer — that is, prayer without special form or at any set time or place. In Biblical times, when the worship of God usually took the form of sacrifices, informal prayers would often be recited during such offerings. Many of these come from the Bible. Of course at that time a prayer book was not yet necessary.

It is useful to remember that the Israelites were perhaps the first people ever to set up definite times for worship, as we saw in connection with Temple offerings, which used to be made every morning, afternoon, and evening. This regularity of worship later led to the need for prayer books.

After the destruction of the First Temple in 586 B.C.E., when most of the Jews were exiled to Babylonia, another place of worship had to be discovered besides the Temple. The synagogue was born and began to grow as an accepted institution not only in Babylonia, but even in Israel, after the return there following the end of the exile.

The earliest established prayer was the *Shema*, which every Jew was supposed to know by heart. After the return of the Jews to their homeland, Ezra and the 120 members of the Great Synagogue composed the *Amidah*. Ezra believed that the Jews should have a definite prayer through which they could adequately express themselves to

God. He was also concerned that people who had been born in Babylonia and who did not know Hebrew very well might forget the language unless they used it daily in prayer.

As people began to pray in the synagogues as well as in the Temple, they felt the need for a prayer book and found it necessary to have prayers written down instead of merely recited by heart. Furthermore, as the number of synagogues increased, it became necessary to maintain some measure of uniformity by the use of the same written prayer book. Torah study had also become part of the service, and in this way special prayers connected with the Torah reading came into being.

Even though the basic order of our prayers had already been established over fifteen hundred years ago, or around 400 C.E., there still did not exist any regular *Siddur* with the prayers arranged in a definite order until the time of Rabbi Amram Gaon of Babylonia who lived during the ninth century C.E. The Jewish community of Barcelona, Spain, had once asked Rabbi Amram to prepare for them a systematic outline of the order of the prayers to be recited throughout the year. This draft became the framework of the *Siddur* we use today.

Many other *Siddurim* then followed, the best known of which were those of Rashi (the noted Bible commentator who lived during the

"Blessing of the Children on the Sabbath Eve," by Moritz Oppenheim.

eleventh and twelfth centuries), Moses Maimonides (the most famous of Jewish medieval scholars), and the *Maḥzor Vitry*, written by Rabbi Simḥah of Vitry, France, one of Rashi's students. However, these *Siddurim* contain the same general framework as that of Rabbi Amram's *Siddur* and of our *Siddurim* of the present day. The invention of printing in the fifteenth century also led to uniformity of content in the *Siddur*.

Certain differences, however, arose in the versions of the prayers used by Jews in different countries. The Jews of most European countries followed what is known as the Ashkenazic version (style) or order of prayers, while the Jews of southern Europe, North Africa, and Asia followed the Sephardic version. The main distinction between the two usually consisted of a different arrangement of some of the prayers, or the addition of special prayers into the *Siddur*.

Nowadays, each branch of Judaism — Orthodox, Conservative, and Reform — also has its special *Siddur* for its worshippers. The Orthodox *Siddur* is, of course, the traditional one, containing the prayers in their complete form, just as they were handed down from earliest times. The Conservative prayer book includes most of the prayers, omits some of them, and makes changes in others.

The Reform, or "Union" prayer book, has always differed from the first two in many ways. For one thing, it is much shorter. It also contains less Hebrew and more English. However, just recently, the latest edition of the Reform *Siddur*, entitled *Gates of Prayer*, contains more Hebrew than it ever did, and in it you will also find certain kinds of prayers that before were simply not found in a Reform prayer book. Among these newly introduced prayers are those for the State of Israel, blessings over the *lulav* and *etrog*, blessings for *Havdalah*, and even those for the *tallit* and *tefillin*.

The Jewish Reconstructionist Society, founded by Dr. Mordecai Kaplan, has also published a prayer book that retains many of the traditional prayers, but has made some fundamental changes in others.*

SOME OF THE SIDDUR'S BEST-KNOWN PRAYERS

Although every prayer is sacred to us because it is directed to God, there are a few that are of outstanding interest.

1) The Amidah

As we have mentioned earlier, there are a few different names for this prayer. It is most popularly known as the *Shemoneh Essrei*, which means "eighteen blessings," although it actually contains nineteen, an extra one having been added about two thousand years ago. The name *Amidah* itself means "standing," which is how we are meant to recite it.

---

*Additional information on different types of *Siddurim* can be found in P. Arian and A. Eisenberg's *The Story of the Prayerbook*, pp. 114-130.

In Talmudic times, the *Amidah* was known simply as *Tefillah* (meaning "*the* prayer") because it was regarded as the most significant prayer of all.

The *Amidah* is said at least three times daily throughout the year. On ordinary weekdays it is said during the morning, afternoon, and evening services. On Sabbaths and festivals it is said a fourth time — during the *Musaf*, or "additional" service — and on *Yom Kippur* it is said a fifth time for the *Neilah*, or "closing" service.

You have already been told that the *Amidah* was composed by Ezra the Scribe and the Scholars of the Great Synagogue after the return of the Jews from the Babylonian exile. The three major ideas of the *Amidah* — praise, petition, and thanksgiving — were intended to serve as a framework for later prayers and as a guideline for a possible way to recite private prayer.

The middle part of the *Amidah* — the thirteen paragraphs of petition — is omitted on Sabbaths and festivals because dwelling on our day-to-day needs may make us feel sad. Instead, we substitute prayers and blessings that are special to those holy days.

If you were to walk into a synagogue while the congregation was reciting the *Amidah*, you would see the worshippers standing, facing east (toward Jerusalem), praying silently, and occasionally bending forward. Why? Because each person feels that he is standing before the Almighty, directly facing Him. It is only in a position of such honor and respect that a Jew could ever think of coming before God to praise Him, thank Him, and ask Him to grant certain requests.

Following the silent prayer of the congregants, the Reader repeats the *Amidah* aloud (except during the evening prayer). In this way everybody is given the opportunity to hear just how this prayer sounds when read correctly. Thus, even those who cannot read properly are at least able to answer *Amen* after the repetition of each blessing.

There are appropriate additions made to the *Amidah* on Sabbaths, festivals, new moons, and other times. On *Rosh Ḥodesh* (new moon), a

"Blessing of the Sabbath Candles,"
woodcut, Amsterdam, 18th century.

125

Jews at prayer in the synagogue. Miniature from the Mahzor Lipsia, Germany, 14th century.

special insertion is made in the third portion of the *Amidah,* "thanksgiving." Also, in the *Musaf* (additional) service for Sabbaths and festivals, the middle section deals with the sacrifices that used to be offered in the Temple on those particular holidays, and also expresses the hope that someday the Temple will be rebuilt and the sacrifices restored.

2) The Shema

Of all our prayers, this is the oldest and perhaps the most holy. The *Shema* is, however, not really a prayer, but a declaration of belief in God and that God is One (Deuteronomy 6:4-9).

Although all three portions of the *Shema* are recited during the *Shaḥarit* (morning) and the *Arvit* (evening) services, segments of this prayer are also said during other parts of the service.

When we openly declare our belief in God and that God is One, we mean that we accept Him as the divine Ruler over our lives and that to God and God alone do we remain steadfast and faithful; we accept the rule of no other god. This belief is the most basic part of our faith and enables us to live and function as Jews.

It was because of this belief that so many Jews, during times of bitter persecution and when given the choice between accepting another religion or death, chose to die rather than give up their Judaism. Their last words before death were:

Shema Yisrael, Hashem Elokaynu, Hashem Ehad!

"Hear, O Israel, The Lord is Our God, the Lord is One!"

After this opening line comes the affirmation of God's sovereignty: "Blessed be His name, whose glorious kingdom is for ever and ever." There then follow three more paragraphs:

126

a) (Deuteronomy 6:5-9)

We must love God and be faithful to Him. We must always remember His commandments; we must teach them to our children and keep them in mind in every act of our lives, from the time we wake up in the morning until we go to bed at night. Next, by the commandment to wear *tefillin* upon our arm and upon our head, we are supposed to remember that we are Jews. Finally comes the law of placing a *mezuzah* upon the doorpost of our house.

b) (Deuteronomy 11:13-21)

Here we are given the choice of either following God's laws and enjoying happiness and prosperity, or disobeying them and suffering the consequences. The forms of punishment mentioned — famine and exile — are described in greater detail than are the blessings, so as to warn us against making the wrong choice.

The four species used in the festival of Suk-kot — the etrog, palm, myrtle and willow — in the hands of hassidic boy. Painting by Isidor Kaufman.

The commandments of *tefillin* and *mezuzah* and the obligation to teach Torah to children, all of which were mentioned in the first paragraph, are repeated here.

c) (Numbers 15:37-41)

Most of this paragraph covers the commandments of *tzitzit*, and closes with an additional reminder that when God took the Jewish people out of Egypt, it was on the condition that they accepted Him as their God.

The *tzitzit*, according to Rashi's explanation, are a reminder of all the 613 commandments contained in the Torah. The numerical value of the word *tzitzit* amounts to 600, and eight threads and five knots on each fringe make up the remaining thirteen, totaling 613.

As has already been mentioned, the *Shema* is recited only twice daily (in the morning "when you rise up," and in the evening "when you lie down"). It is not said in the afternoon. However, before going to sleep at night, we do say the first paragraph of the *Shema*.*

The distinct message of each of the three paragraphs of the *Shema* is now clear to us: we are called upon to enrich our lives by remembering God and His commandments.

3) The Aleinu

At the end of each service — *Shaḥarit*, *Minḥa*, and *Arvit* — the congregation always sings or says the *Aleinu*. Even if someone has already said this prayer quietly, he must join in again when it is read aloud in the synagogue.

The *Aleinu* begins by thanking God for having made us Jews who worship One God, as distinct from other peoples who practice idolatry. At the words *Va'anaḥnu kor'im*, "for we kneel and bow down before the supreme King of Kings, the Holy One, blessed be He," we bend our knees and bow forward slightly.

In the second paragraph we express the hope that the day will soon come when all peoples will recognize the authority of God as the One and only God and, in so doing, will also feel the bonds of true human brotherhood.

According to tradition, this prayer is said to have originated in the time of Joshua, who led the Jewish people into the Promised Land. He taught them to sing the *Aleinu* so as to remind them that they must behave completely differently from the peoples they would come in contact with when they entered Canaan (Israel).

This prayer actually came into regular practice at the time of Rav, a famous Babylonian scholar who lived during the third century C.E. He inserted the *Aleinu* into that part of the *Rosh Hashanah* service in which we proclaim God's royalty over the universe. It is a tragic fact that during the Middle Ages the *Aleinu*, which extols the unity of all people, was used as an excuse for attacks against our ancestors.

At that time the Christians persecuted and murdered the Jews

*For additional information on the *Shema*, see N. Mindel, *My Prayer*, pp. 152-168.

Title page of a prayer book,
with translations in the German language,
printed in Amsterdam in 1705.

continually. Around the twelfth century, some Jewish apostates turned on their own people and accused them of making insulting references to Christians in their prayers. They used the *Aleinu* as a case in point. What offended the Gentiles most was not so much the words "who has not made us like other nations . . ." but another verse that had once followed them, which read, ". . . they worship vain things and emptiness, and pray to a god that cannot save" (Isaiah 45:20).

As a matter of fact, this latter verse had already existed as a part of the *Aleinu* prayer of the High Holy Day service in the time of Rav, when it referred to actual idol worshippers in Babylonia, where there were no Christians at that period. The rabbis tried to explain this to their accusers, but to no avail. Many Jews were burned at the stake because of the attacks against the *Aleinu*. Yet, even while dying, they were heard to sing the familiar melody of the prayer that had been used as an excuse to send them to their death. They thus ended their lives proclaiming their belief in the One God.

In the end, in spite of the Jews' insistence on the true meaning of the verse under dispute, it had to be deleted from the *Aleinu*, and it no longer appears in the Ashkenazic *Siddur*. The Sephardic prayer book, however, never removed it, so it can still be found there.

129

The second paragraph of the *Aleinu* makes it quite clear that the purpose of the prayer is not to insult non-Jews, but rather, first, to remind us of the martyrs who had suffered for the beliefs contained in this prayer, and, above all, to express our hope that the belief in God will someday unite all peoples in true brotherhood and mutual friendship.

This second paragraph thus shows us that, although a feeling of bitterness toward non-Jews would have been perfectly understandable in light of the continuous and seemingly unending persecutions the Jew had to suffer at the hands of the non-Jews in the Middle Ages, the hatred that our people were enduring meant less to them than the hope of some future bond of human brotherhood.

When the *Aleinu* is recited during the *Musaf* service on *Rosh Hashanah* and *Yom Kippur*, the rabbi, the cantor, and many congregants kneel as a sign of faith and loyalty to God.

Since the twelfth century, probably because it is meant to serve as a reminder of the martyrdom of our medieval ancestors, the *Aleinu* has become a regular part of our daily prayers, to be recited at the close of each service.

As a result of reciting this prayer three times a day and saying it in its more dramatic form on the High Holy Days, we are constantly reminded that man's power is nothing as compared with God's and that we owe our deepest loyalty to Him alone.

4) The Ashrei

We recite the *Ashrei* three times a day, twice during *Shaharit* and once at the beginning of *Minha*. Most of this prayer comes from Psalm 145. Why does it occupy such a prominent place in the service?

As it reads in Hebrew, the first letter of every verse of the *Ashrei* follows in alphabetical order. There appear to be a few reasons for this arrangement. First, the alphabetical order is an easy way of remembering a prayer whose meaning does not otherwise follow a set order. Second, the *Ashrei* aims to teach us that "God's praise is sung using all the letters, meaning, all possible forms of human expression."*

An outstanding verse in this prayer is, "You open Your hand and satisfy each creature with favor." Here we are told that God takes care of, and is concerned for, each of His creatures.

Our rabbis thought so much of this prayer that they said that "whoever says (it) three times daily will have a share in the world to come" (Berakhot 4b). All the letters of the Hebrew alphabet are represented by the first letter of each succeeding verse, except for the *nun*. Our rabbis believed that when King David composed this Psalm, he must have foreseen a verse from Amos (5:2) that begins with the word *naflah* (meaning "fallen"), and he therefore did not want to include that verse in the Psalm. However, there is some comfort for the "fallen" in the verse that immediately succeeds the missing one begin-

*N. Mindel, p. 126.

ning with *nun*, which reads: "The Lord upholds all who fall and raises up all who are bowed down." From this we see that God does not want those who fall to remain down, but to rise up and be able to take their place as equals among all men.

5) Special Prayers for Special Days

a) The Penitential Prayers

After the *Amidah* for *Shaharit* and *Minhah* on weekdays, Tah-anun, a short penitential prayer asking forgiveness of sins, is said. On Mondays and Thursdays the longer portion, beginning with the words *vehu rahum*, is added. On Sabbaths, festivals, new moons, and certain other days, all forms of these penitential prayers are omitted because of their very serious nature.

b) Sabbath and festivals

Special prayers are said on Sabbaths and festivals, in addition to most of the weekday prayers.

c) New Moons

Prayers that relate to *Rosh Hodesh* are said on this day, especially during the *Musaf* service.

d) Fast Days

Still other special prayers are added on all minor fasts and on the Fast of *Av*.

e) Special *Selihot* (penitential prayers)

We begin reciting these several days before *Rosh Hashanah* and continue until *Yom Kippur*.

6) The Various Blessings

As well as the blessings we say before eating foods like fruit or bread, or when drinking wine, or for any other food, there are a number that are recited on particular occasions, such as when washing hands before a meal, on seeing a rainbow, on hearing good news, when wearing an article of clothing for the first time, and for many others. An observant Jew will usually recite as many as one hundred blessings every day.

The prayers mentioned above are only some of the better-known ones. A few others include the *Kaddish*; the prayers in connection with the removal of the Torah from the Ark and its return; the Torah blessings; the prayers which preceded and follow the *Shema*; the Grace after meals, and the night prayers.

FORMS OF PRAYER BOOKS

Although the most commonly used prayer book is the *Siddur*, there are other books that a Jew uses to pray from on certain occasions. For each major festival (*Pesah*, *Shavuot*, *Sukkot*, and the High Holy Days) there is a special prayer book called a *Mahzor*, which contains all the regular and special prayers for that particular festival, as well as related Torah readings and other material, such as the customs, laws, poems, songs, and so forth.

So, for example, in a *Sukkot Maḥzor* will be found, in addition to the prayers usually recited for every festival, the laws pertaining to the use of the *etrog* and *lulav*, the special prayers for entering a *sukkah*, as well as those for *Shemini Atzeret* and *Simḥat Torah*, and all the Torah and *Haftorah* readings.

Although the *Haggadah* of *Pesaḥ* is used for the first two nights only, it contains many prayers and hymns that are also recited on other occasions.

Another special booklet is the *Kinot*, containing the special prayers and readings for *Tisha b'Av* (the Fast of *Av*). Yet another is the *Seliḥot* booklet in which are found the special penitential prayers for the various fasts.

Although the Book of Psalms (the *Tehillim*) is not a prayerbook, it is read during, before, or after some of the services and is sometimes printed in a separate booklet.

SOME OTHER MATTERS PERTAINING TO PRAYER

1. Singing

Prayers are sung, as well as read or spoken, in the synagogue. The cantor chants the prayers as he leads the service, and the congregation also often chants out loud. There is a great deal of community singing in the service, in which a certain melody is sung in unison.

As well as making the service more enjoyable, singing helps us to remember the words better.

Singing has been an important part of the service ever since the Temple days, when the *Kohanim* would perform the service as some Levites sang and others played special musical instruments.

2. Bodily Movements

A Jew often makes use of his entire body, as well as his lips and his voice, to pray. He does not remain rigid and seated all the time. Certain prayers, for example the *Amidah* and the *Aleinu*, are to be said standing. Also, during certain parts of the *Amidah* and the *Aleinu*, we bend the knee and lean forward slightly as a sign of reverence before God.

During the *Amidah* we remain on our feet because it is as if we were standing directly before God, in true reverence. We take three steps back and three steps forward again, at the beginning of this prayer, as a sign of greeting the King. Instead of turning our backs at the end of the *Amidah*, we take three steps back to show how humbly we take leave of our Master, before Whom we have come. When we recite this prayer, we stand at attention, keeping both feet together as a reminder of the angels mentioned in the opening chapter of Ezekiel (1:7) who have "straight feet."

Jews often sway backward and forward and make other bodily motions while praying as expressions of their inner feelings. Ḥassidim often break out into dance during prayer.

3. Regularity of Worship

The recitation of prayers at set times in the morning, afternoon, and evening is supposed to become a regular habit every day of the year. Just as eating and sleeping are important for physical and mental health, so does regularity of prayer fulfill a basic spiritual need.

4. A Few Rules of Conduct

During prayer there are certain rules of conduct that must be observed. Among them are: Do not talk or whisper; do not do anything distracting; do nothing that might seem disrespectful. We

Title page of Salamone de Rossi's synagogal compositions "Hashirim asher l'Shelomo," published in Venice in 1623.

should behave as well as, if not better than, we do while talking to someone for whom we have a deep respect. A Hebrew saying goes as follows: "Know before Whom you are standing," referring, of course, to God.

UNDERSTANDING THE MEANING OF PRAYERS

Is there any use in prayer if we do not understand Hebrew? Understanding what the words of a prayer mean does not in itself make the prayer any more effective. On the other hand, if we do not understand a single word of a prayer, but if we pray primarily out of a genuine devotion, the prayer will be effective even without our knowledge of what it means. What is essential to prayer are the feeling and the sincerity behind it, and these are what God listens to.

Ignorance of the meaning of a prayer, however, can and should be remedied. There are prayer books with translations to help you learn what the prayers are saying. At the same time, every effort should be made to learn Hebrew so that you will be able to understand not only many of the prayers but also much of our glorious heritage written in Hebrew. But we must remember that prayer is primarily the "service of the heart." Therefore, whether or not you understand all of the words, be sure that your heart is in your prayers.

There are a few prayers (such as the Confessional of *Yom Kippur* and the *Kapparot* for the eve of *Yom Kippur*) that may be said in any language which a person understands. But this practice has been permitted only for specific prayers, for specific reasons, and is not allowed on a regular basis.

Hebrew is considered the best language for prayer both because the Hebrew prayers are the only ones that have survived and because Hebrew gives them a holiness that does not belong to any other language. Hebrew is especially sacred; it is the "holy tongue" in which the Torah and other Jewish sacred literature are written. Remember, too, that reciting our prayers in Hebrew binds us to our glorious past and unites Jews all over the world in a common language.

SOME OF THE VALUES OF PRAYER

Prayer brings us closer to God because we are speaking directly to Him, either formally or informally, when we pray. Because we pray for one another rather than for ourselves, our prayers are usually expressed in the plural, not in the singular, form. So when we pray, we say, "O God, and God of *our* fathers" instead of "of *my* fathers." In this way, when we pray as Jews and as part of the Jewish community, we are also brought much closer to one another.

The *Siddur* is used for learning as well as for praying. First, the repetition of the Hebrew words becomes a part of us. At the same time, we also get to know something about the Bible in the original, about the Talmud, and about other great pieces of Jewish literature. This, in turn, reminds us that we are descendants of a nation that refuses to die because it has so much to live for.

Elijah announcing the arrival of the Messiah. Woodcut from the Mantuba Haggadah, 1561.

But prayer also has a lasting effect on one's character. While praising and thanking God, we actually learn why we should be grateful to Him. It is He who has given us life and all the good things of life, who protects us against harm and is there to turn to in a time of need.

Remember, also, that trying to improve the way we live our lives should always be one of the main goals of our prayer. Prayer can change our whole frame of mind and the way we live our lives when we leave the synagogue. It can make each one of us a different person.

Still another value of prayer is the sense of true joy and happiness that comes to us as we pray. Putting our trust in God through prayer grants us peace of mind and leaves us with the inner feeling that God has answered us.

From what has been written here, it is clear that prayer makes you a more complete individual as well as a loyal Jew.

Everything that is connected with prayer — including reading, attending synagogue, thinking about God, speaking to Him, learning from the prayers — all of these actions as you perform them will enable you to be a well-rounded Jew, one for whom prayer is a joyful experience.

At the beginning of the chapter we were told to "serve the Lord with joy." That joy can best be experienced when we have learned what prayer is, why we pray, and what we can gain from it — which is what this chapter has tried to demonstrate.

Prayer, then, is yet another way of enjoying our Judaism, because we have made it an integral part of our daily life.

JEWISH BURIAL AND MOURNING CUSTOMS

It is not enough to learn only about the joyful side of Jewish life. We must also understand the laws that have to do with death and mourning, for the following reasons:

1) Since the life cycle of man is not complete without death, and since it is essential to know how death affects us, we cannot **ignore** this part of the human, and the Jewish, experience. Just as we learn the Jewish laws covering every aspect of living, so must we also learn about death.

2) Since death is such an inevitable fact of life, all of us come into contact with it through people who at some time or other are in our lives; that is why it is so necessary for you to have some knowledge of the customs related to death, burial, and mourning, and the reasons for them. Above all, this knowledge will help you to appreciate the effect of these customs on the living.

3) Furthermore, you will discover that every custom regarding death followed by us Jews is somehow connected with our living habits and our relationships with one another.

For example, when a Jew observes a week of mourning for someone close to him, he does so to show respect for the dead person. Also, the *Kaddish* prayer is recited to make the mourner feel that, no matter how deeply he is grieving the loss of a loved one, he still believes in God and in the justice of His action. So he praises and glorifies God, instead of feeling bitter.

4) Through a correct understanding of the meaning underlying the customs connected with death and mourning and behaving in the way they suggest, you will find yourself showing the same respect for the living as for the dead.

To us Jews it is life, and what we do during our lives, that is far more important to us than death. Much as we respect the dead and those they have left behind, the purpose of this chapter is to explain how each custom is closely related to our everyday living habits and to our attitudes toward other people.

In fact, you will notice that all these customs are based, fundamentally, on the following two principles:

1) To show the necessary honor and respect for the deceased, and
2) To care about the feelings of the survivors and to try to help and comfort them in every way possible during their time of need.

Therefore, it may be said that as we study how to treat the dead, we can learn how we should act toward the living.

AS DEATH DRAWS NEAR

We Jews are a people who never lose hope as long as there is even the least sign of life in a human being. We believe God can save the sick until the very end of his or her life.

There are various ways in which we express this. First, as soon as it appears that death is near, certain Psalms are recited in the synagogue, especially Psalm 119, in which the first letter of every verse is in alphabetical order. We then read those verses whose first letter corresponds to the Hebrew name of the dying person, and we pray that God will save him. Members of the family and others then add their own prayers.

As soon as it seems that the person has hardly much longer to live, he is asked to recite the *Viduy* or "Confession," in which he also prays for life, but accepts whatever is God's will with love. His closing words are those of the *Shema:*

"Hear, O Israel, the Lord is our God, the Lord is One."

In this way the dying person maintains his full faith in God until the very end.

WHEN DEATH FINALLY COMES

As soon as all signs of life have left the body, all those who are present recite the words, *Barukh Dayan emet,* "Blessed be the Judge of truth," in this way demonstrating their acceptance of God's will with courage and faith.

Following this, all close relatives make a small rip in a part of their outer garments as a sign of grief. This ceremony is known as *keriah* ("tearing"), to show that, unfortunately, the deceased has been torn away from the living. However, both of these customs — *Barukh Dayan emet* and *keriah* — are nowadays usually conducted at the cemetery just before the burial. The *keriah* ceremony is never performed on Sabbaths or festivals, nor are clothes that have been torn in this way to be worn on any of these holy days.

Then begins the sacred task of preparing the body for burial. This is usually done by the members of the *Ḥevrah Kaddisha* (the "Holy

Brotherhood" or "Burial Society"), usually made up of devout and observant Jews.

The body must be bathed and cleaned (a ritual known as *taharah*, or "purity") and prepared for burial. Plain white linen *takhrikhim*, or "shrouds," are used for everyone, to show that rich and poor, high and low, are equal in death. A man is usually clothed in a *tallit*, one fringe of which is torn, signifying that this holy garment is no longer to be used.

From the time of death until burial, the corpse is never to be left alone, which further shows respect for the departed. Someone, preferably a relative, should stay with the deceased and recite Psalms.

The old Jewish cemetery in Worms. At left: tombstone of the Maharil, 1427.

At home all pictures, mirrors, or any other ornaments are either covered or taken away. A large candle is kept burning continuously for the entire *shiva* period.

THE BURIAL

The burial ceremony should take place as soon after death as possible, usually within twenty-four hours (except on Sabbaths and festivals), unless a delay is necessary for the arrival of close members of the family. To delay the burial longer than necessary would show disrespect for the dead.

It is generally the custom to hold a brief service in a funeral parlor before the burial. The rabbi will recite a few prayers and Psalms, and will say a few words in honor of the dead. If the deceased was a prominent member of the congregation, the funeral service is usually held in the synagogue, where, in addition to the rabbi, other people in public life may also speak words of praise for the dead. Such a talk is known as a *hesped*, or "eulogy."

It is a great *mitzvah* to join a funeral procession. In fact, such an act is called a *hesed shel emet*, "an act of true kindness," one done out of genuine feeling, since no reward can be expected from the dead.

The burial service is a simple one. The rabbi, or the cantor, again recites a few Psalms and prayers. After the casket has been lowered

Cup for Burial Society (Hevrah Kaddisha), Bohemia, 1692.

into the ground and covered with dirt (which a few relatives and friends of the deceased help to shovel into the grave), the sons (or close relatives) then recite the *Kaddish*.

As the mourners leave the grave, all others present stand in two lines and comfort them as they pass, with the words: "May the Lord comfort you among the other mourners of Zion and Jerusalem."

On leaving the cemetery, all who have attended the burial wash their hands. This custom is a reminder of the Biblical law that one should cleanse oneself after having contact with the dead.

THE SHIVA PERIOD

Following the burial service, there begin three periods of mourning: the *shiva*, the *sheloshim*, and the twelve-month *avelut* period.

Immediately after the burial service, the family returns home and begins to "sit *shiva*," or to observe the seven-day period of mourning. The first full meal eaten by the mourners is prepared for them by neighbors or friends. This is another way of showing sympathy for them. The mourners sit on low benches or stools and wear no leather footwear. They are not allowed to do any work, nor is any of them permitted to leave the house during this *shiva* period, except in an emergency.*

Anybody who has lost one of the following close relatives is considered to be a mourner and must sit *shiva:* a father or mother, wife or husband, son or daughter, brother or sister.

During the week of the *shiva*, the prayer services are usually held at the home of the mourners, first, as a sign of respect for the departed, and also to make things easier for them. If, however, a *minyan* (ten adult men) cannot be held in their home, they may go to the synagogue.

During these services the mourners recite the *Kaddish;* even if a son is still a minor, that is, below age thirteen, he is required to say *Kaddish* for the departed parent. A daughter does not have to recite *Kaddish*, although she may answer "Amen," or even recite the prayer quietly to herself, especially if there is no son. The *Kaddish* is recited during each of the three mourning periods.

Shiva is not observed on Sabbaths or festivals, although a holy day is counted as one of the seven *shiva* days. It is a *mitzvah* to visit the mourners during the *shiva* week to comfort them and make them feel that others care for them and their loss.**

THE PERIOD OF SHELOSHIM

The first thirty days following death mark a special mourning period, during which a few of the observances of the *shiva* period are still maintained. Going to school or to work is allowed after the *shiva*, and the regular daily routine of living can be resumed. However, one

*Maurice Lamm, *The Jewish Way in Death and Mourning*, p. 116 ff.
**For additional observances connected with the *shiva*, see Lamm, pp. 77-144.

The tomb of Rachel, at the entrance to Bethlehem.

Tomb of one of the Patriarchs in the Machpelah.

may not listen to music or attend social gatherings, even if no music is played there. But meetings or gatherings that do not include any form of entertainment may be attended during the *sheloshim*.

Some additional restrictions are observed during the *sheloshim* period. These apply to:

1) The wearing of new clothes.
2) Shaving or getting a haircut.
3) Taking part in any festivities, including weddings, circumcisions, and *Pidyon ha-Ben* meals, except for the birth of one's own child.
4) Getting married.

At the close of *sheloshim*, the period of mourning is over for any relative who is not a parent, for whom mourning continues for twelve months.

AVELUT — THE TWELVE-MONTH PERIOD

A person mourning the death of a father or mother is called an *Avel*, and he is required to observe this period of mourning (known as *avelut*) for twelve months, beginning from the day of the parent's death.

Throughout the entire one-year period some of the restrictions observed during *shiva* and *sheloshim* (such as parties, dances, music, and the like) are still in force. The *Kaddish* is recited for eleven months and not for the full year. The Talmud teaches that the wicked are judged for a whole year, and since we do not usually consider our parents to have been wicked, this prayer is therefore said only for eleven months, less one day.

We mourn for parents for a full year because of the love and respect we have for their memory and because of our gratitude for the sacrifices they made for us while they were alive. When sadness at such a great loss is still fresh, it is unlikely that one would even want to enjoy oneself.

But, on the other hand, it is not the Jewish way to mourn for a departed parent for more than one year, since such behavior would ap-

141

pear as though the mourner were regarding death to be more important to him than life. Such an attitude is contrary to Jewish belief.

One of the best ways of showing love and respect for a departed parent is to try to live by those fine qualities for which he or she is remembered. If a father or mother used to give a lot of money to charity and was very kind to people, his or her memory will live on if the children do the same. There is no doubt that this would have been the wish of the parent during his or her lifetime.

THE YAHRZEIT

The *Yahrzeit* (memorial anniversary), which may be observed for any departed relative, and especially for parents, lasts from sundown to sundown and is observed as follows:

1) A special memorial candle, lit just before dusk on the eve of the *Yahrzeit*, is kept burning until the evening of the following day.

2) Sons attend synagogue services, where they recite the *Kaddish*. If possible, one of them may also lead the services during that day.

3) It is also customary if possible for the mourners to fast on this day — at least to refrain from eating meat or drinking wine. This is another way of showing respect for the departed.

4) Studying Torah and giving money to charity are also done on the anniversary of the *Yahrzeit*. The learning may consist of going over a portion of the Torah, the Mishnah, or some other holy books (in Hebrew or in English).

5) On the Sabbath before the *Yahrzeit*, or even on the day of the *Yahrzeit* itself if it falls on a Sabbath, Monday or Thursday, when the Torah is read, the *El Molei Raḥamim* prayer is recited. Both the name of the departed and the name of his or her father are mentioned in this prayer.

Alms box, shaped like tombstone and grave, with inscription, "Righteousness delivereth from death," Germany, 1825.

*Destroyed tombstones of the famous
cemetery of Mount Olive, Jerusalem, used by
Arabs to build fences around their homes.*

6) On the Sabbath, Monday, or Thursday of the *Yahrzeit*, the mourner is usually called upon for an *aliyah* (Torah honor).

7) Finally, it is also customary to visit the grave of the departed as a sign of respect. Here, Psalms may be recited and the *El Molei Raḥamim* prayer chanted.

In addition to the annual *Yahrzeit*, the departed are also remembered on *Yom Kippur*, *Shemini Atzeret*, the last day of Passover, and the second day of *Shavuot*. On each of these days the special *Yizkor* memorial prayer is recited, as well as the *El Molei Raḥamim*.

THE TOMBSTONE UNVEILING

Within the first year following the death it is customary to set up a tombstone at the head of the grave of the departed and to hold a special "unveiling" ceremony.

On this occasion the family, relatives, and friends gather in the cemetery at the graveside, where the tombstone is covered with a cloth. Before the unveiling, the rabbi, cantor, or some other learned man will usually recite several Psalms and speak a few words of praise in honor of the deceased. After the veil (or cloth) is removed, the person who is conducting the service will chant *El Molei Raḥamim*, followed by the *Kaddish*, during which there must be at least a *minyan* present.

143

Praying at the tomb of Maimonides in Tiberias.

Even though a tombstone need not be erected at the grave, its presence honors the dead by marking the place of burial, making everybody who visits that spot aware of who is buried there and offering a further sign of respect by the survivors.

Why is the tombstone put up about a year after death? Before that time, while the mourners' thoughts were constantly on the death of their loved one, no other reminder was necessary. When the year of mourning is over, the tombstone remains as a permanent monument. However, if desired, a tombstone may be set up sooner than that, or at any time following *sheloshim.*

THE KADDISH

We have mentioned the *Kaddish* prayer several times, but if you read its translation, you will find no mention of death in it. Why, then, is it recited after someone has died?

The *Kaddish* is an important prayer recited in five different forms (including the Mourner's Kaddish). It is recited about thirteen times during the synagogue services, usually to mark a transition in the service.

Basically, the *Kaddish* has nothing to do with death. It is a prayer magnifying the Name of God. However, the person who has, God forbid, just lost a father, mother, or anyone else who is close and dear to him, has need of just that kind of prayer to take him out of himself and to relieve his feelings. He may secretly be asking himself if it was fair of God to take away a person he loved so much. It is just when such a thought occurs to the mourner that he should stand and proclaim, *YITGADAL V'YITKADASH,* "Magnified and sanctified be His Great Name . . ." By expressing himself in this way, he shows that he still believes in the justice of God's ways.

144

Charity box, Altona, Germany, 1854.

When the mourner stands and recites this memorial prayer three times daily throughout the year, the shock of death that he has suffered will become easier to bear. And as he studies the meaning of the words of the *Kaddish*, he will find in them certain lessons about death and life that will also comfort him.

The *Kaddish*, which is said for eleven months, must be recited in the presence of a *minyan*. This, too, helps the mourner because it is only when others are present that he is able to sense that his fellow man shares his grief. This realization eases his pain, and, as a result, he does not feel as lonely as he might have otherwise.

Furthermore, as people see the mourner repeat the *Kaddish* on a regular basis, day by day, they realize how devoted he is to the departed — because he shows respect to that person's memory at so much effort to himself. This act, then, becomes an even greater tribute to the departed.

If you study the words of the *Kaddish*, you will notice that the language in which it is written is not Hebrew, but Aramaic, a language akin to Hebrew. Thousands of years ago Aramaic was the language of the common people, and for this reason the *Kaddish* was originally conceived in its original Aramaic, so that every Jew would understand it better.

HONORING THE DECEASED AFTER DEATH

Here is a brief summary of a few ways in which we honor the departed, especially after the first year, so that they will always be remembered and loved.

1) By observing the *Yahrzeit* each year and by reciting *Yizkor* on the festivals; by following the rules mentioned in connection with these observances, and especially the *Kaddish*.

2) By naming a newborn child after the deceased.

3) By making donations to some Jewish charity in the name of the deceased.

4) By making every effort to live up to the best qualities that characterized the departed so that they can live on as an inspiration. For example, if the deceased is remembered for his or her patience, kindness, or sincerity, the son, daughter, or relative should also try to

develop these same traits, not only for the memory of the departed but for his or her own benefit as well.

WHAT HAS LEARNING ABOUT DEATH AND MOURNING TAUGHT US?

The customs connected with death can teach us a lot about our relations with one another and how we can improve our conduct and character through them. Here are a few examples of how such improvement can be brought about.

We have seen how every effort is made to prolong the life of the person who is about to die, even when death is imminent. It is because life itself is so precious to us that we spare no effort to keep that person alive, even though it may seem that all reason for hope is gone. In other words, we Jews never give up hope, because we value life too highly to do so.

Whenever we take part in a funeral procession, that is one way of showing our sincerity. We certainly do not expect thanks or reward from the dead.

After the funeral, friends and neighbors flock to the home of the deceased to prepare the first meal for the mourners. They do this because they realize how helpless that family is at a time of such grief. This shows understanding for the feelings of the mourners.

The son's regular observance of the *Kaddish*, throughout the first year and then at every *Yahrzeit* after that, is a genuine demonstration of his devotion to his departed parent. Also, when any Jew gives the proper congregational responses to the *Kaddish*, he is showing that he shares the mourner's grief.

The few customs reviewed here are excellent examples of certain ways of developing character, such as demonstrating the value of human life, performing an act out of sincerity, helping others when the needs arises, expressing devotion to parents, and, finally, sharing someone else's feelings.

Certainly, it is just at such a time that we are most likely to feel kindly toward the departed person, and it is perfectly natural for such feelings to be aroused when death strikes. But why should we wait until a tragedy occurs, God forbid, before expressing our deep feelings towards others? Why not practice that same kindness at all times and in every way possible?

Keeping the above in mind, you can see that the Jewish reaction to death shows the high value Judaism places on life. *U-va-ḥar-ta ba-ḥayyim!* "And you shall choose life."

Only the familiar customs connected with burial and mourning have been dealt with in this chapter. Many more, especially those practiced by Jews in other lands, can be read about elsewhere.

All these customs serve the common purpose of ennobling and enriching the lives of the living and of strengthening their Jewish existence.

146

THE MOURNER'S KADDISH

Yit-ga-dal v'yit-ka-dash, Sh'mei rabba

B'alma dee-v'ra khir-ootei v'yam-leekh mal'khoo-tei, b'hay-yei-khon uv'yo-mei-khon uv'hayyei d'khol beit Yisrael, ba-agala uviz-man kareev, v'im-ru Amein.

Y'hei Sh'mei rabba m'varakh, l'al'am ule-al-mei al-mayya.

Yit-barakh v'yish-tab-bakh, v'yit-pa-ar, v'yit-romam, v'yit-nassei, v'yit-haddar, v'yit-alleh, v'yit-hallal, sh'mei d'koo-d'sha, b'reekh Hu.

L'eil'la min kol bir-khata v'sheerata, toosh-b'hata, v'nehemata, da-ameeron b'alma, v'im-ru Amein.

Y'hei sh'lama rabba min Sh'mayya, v'hayyeem aleinu v'al kol Yisrael, v'im-ru Amein.

Oseh shalom bim'romov, Hu ya-aseh shalom aleinu v'al kol Yisrael, v'im-ru Amein.

Glorified and sanctified be God's great name, throughout the world which He has created, according to His will.

May He establish His kingdom in your lifetime and during your days, and within the life of the entire House of Israel, speedily and soon, and let us say AMEN!

May His great name be blessed forever and to all eternity.

Blessed and praised, glorified and exalted, extolled and honored, adored and lauded be the name of the Holy One, blessed be He, beyond all the blessings, hymns, praise, and consolations that are ever spoken in the world; and let us say AMEN!

May there be abundant peace from Heaven, and life for us and for all Israel, and let us say AMEN!

He who creates peace in His heavenly heights, may He create peace for us and for all Israel, and let us say AMEN!

THE HEBREW CALENDAR

THE HEBREW AND CIVIL CALENDARS

Why Do We Jews Have a Calendar That Is Different?

Have you ever wondered why our Jewish holidays are not always on the same day each year in the calendar you use every day?

Thus, why is Passover sometimes in late March or April, but never on the same day every year? To answer this question, you first have to know something about our Hebrew calendar and why and in what ways it differs from the one that hangs on your wall.

How Does Our Calendar Differ From Others?

The basic difference between our Hebrew calendar and the civil calendar in everyday use is that the latter is based on the movements of the *sun* and is therefore called a *solar* calendar. Our Hebrew calendar, on the other hand, is based on the movements of the *moon* and is therefore a *lunar* calendar.

Now, let us take a look at what this basic difference between the two calendars means to us, as we can see from the following figures:

Solar Year: 365 days
Lunar Year: 354 days
11 days difference.

Thus, a solar year consists of 365 days because it takes the earth 365 days to revolve around the sun. But the moon makes its trip around the earth in only 354 days, eleven days less than the earth takes to travel around the sun.

This eleven-day difference, then, makes each day in our lunar calendar come out eleven days earlier than it did the year before. For

Nisan (30 days)

Iyar (29 days)

example, let us suppose that *Rosh Hashanah* (the New Year) would come out as follows:

In 1973 — on September 25
1974 — on September 14
1975 — on September 3
1976 — on August 23

From these dates you can now see how this difference of eleven days between the lunar and solar calendars makes *Rosh Hashanah* come out so much earlier each year. In three years it would arrive over a month earlier.

Why Does This Difference Matter to Us?

Now, this annual change in dates would not matter except for the fact that, since most of our festivals must occur in their proper season every year (Passover in the spring, *Sukkot* in the fall, etc.), we cannot allow a festival to fall too far out of its respective season.

How Is Our Calendar Kept in Order?

The above question might also be worded: What do we do to our lunar dates to keep them from lagging farther and farther behind their proper seasons? A *leap year* is the simple solution to the problem.

In the civil, or solar, calendar, a leap year consists of *one additional day every four years*. (This comes about because there are actually 365¼ days in a solar year, the additional day falling on February 29, every four years.)

In order to balance our Hebrew calendar against the civil year, a leap year occurs every two or three years, consisting of *one additional month*. Let us now compare the leap year in each of the two calendars:

Civil (Solar)	Hebrew (Lunar)
1 additional *day*	1 additional *month*
every *4 years*	every *2 or 3 years*

The reason why a leap year comes every two or three years can be explained by examining the nineteen-year cycle of leap years:

1 2 (3) 4 5 (6) 7 (8) 9 10 (11) 12 13 (14) 15 16 (17) 18 (19)

The following features can be noticed from these figures: First, a leap year falls every third, sixth, eighth, eleventh, fourteenth, seventeenth, and nineteenth year. That is why seven of the nineteen figures are in parentheses, showing that a leap year occurs either every two or three years. Because of these leap years you will also notice that, whenever one of our festivals is very early in a given year (such as

149

Sivan   (30 days)   Tamuz   (29 days)

Rosh Hashanah, which can be as early as September 6 or 7), it will come out much later the following year (sometimes as late as early October). This, then, is the second answer to our opening question — our holidays fall on different days in each solar year not only because of the eleven day difference between the solar and lunar years but also because of the leap years in our lunar calendar.

But How Can We Tell Which Is a Leap Year?

How, then, do we know where our present year is in this nineteen-year cycle? How can we tell when the next leap year will occur? This can be determined by first knowing what the present Jewish year is and then dividing it by nineteen.

Thus, for example, if the present year is 5752, we have: 5752 divided by 19 equaling 302, plus a remainder of 14, which means that during the past 5,752 years there have been 302 full cycles of 19 years each, plus 14 remaining years.

This remainder of fourteen shows us to be at the fourteenth year in the 19-cycle. Referring again to this cycle (above), we can see that this fourteenth year is a leap year. The next two years will be ordinary years (not leap years), but the third year (No. 17) will again be a leap year — in 5755.

THE JEWISH YEAR

Why Are Our Years Numbered Differently?

Not only is there a difference in our Hebrew calendar between the length of a moon year and a sun year, but the method of numbering our years also differs from that of other peoples.

The ancient Greeks used to number their years by beginning their calendar with the date of the First Olympiad (775 B.C.E.*); the Romans of old began from the time of the founding of the city of Rome (about 754 B.C.E.); the Moslems, from the year when Mohammed fled from the city of Mecca (the Hegira, 622 C.E.**); while the Christian years date from the birth of Jesus. Thus, 1979 means that it is 1,979 years since Jesus was born.

But we Jews count our years from the date of the creation of the world, which in the Christian year 1979, is 5739. In this way the year 5739 means that it is 5,739 years since the earth was created.

*B.C.E. — Before the Common Era, used instead of B.C.
**C.E. — Common Era, used instead of A.D.

150

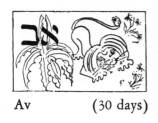

Av   (30 days)

Elul   (29 days)

Of course, even though science tells us that the earth is very much older than this, we still observe this date as part of our tradition as it has been handed down to us.*

By adding 3760 to the number of the Christian year, we can work out the Jewish year. For example, the year 1979 is 5739 in our Hebrew calendar. Similarly, we can subtract 3760 from the Hebrew year to determine the date of the Christian year. Thus, the Hebrew year 5734 is 1974 in the civil calendar.

Why Do Our Jewish Years Differ in Length?

The ordinary Jewish year (that is, when there is no leap year) contains, as we have already seen, 354 days. During a leap year there are 384 days because of the additional month.

OUR HEBREW MONTHS

In our Hebrew calendar there are twelve months (thirteen during a leap year), as follows:

SPRING	SUMMER	FALL	WINTER
Nisan	Tammuz	Tishri	Tevet
Iyar	Av	Heshvan	Sh'vat
Sivan	Elul	Kislev	Adar

(See also table, "The Hebrew and Civil Calendars at a Glance," which can be found at the end of this chapter.)

Since each month contains an average of 29.5 days, it is necessary to add half a day to one month and to deduct half a day from the next month. Therefore, the months usually alternate in length (29 days in one, 30 in the next), and the average length of each month is 29.5 days.

Now, multiply this 29.5 by 12, and you have 354 days in a year. The thirteenth month of each leap year is called *Adar Sheni,* or "the second *Adar.*"

The names of our Hebrew months, as you can see from the above list and the table, are entirely different from those of the civil calendar. In the Five Books of Moses only the month in which the Israelites left

*A number of interpretations have been given to explain this difference. Perhaps the best known among them is the one stating that prior to the creation of the world, countless others before it had been created and destroyed. See Michael Asheri, *Jewish Living.* See also Philip Birnbaum, *A Book of Jewish Concepts,* p. 100.

Tishri   (30 days)

Marheshvan (29 or 30 days)
(Heshvan)

Egypt is mentioned by name — *Aviv* (ripening) — while the others are referred to solely by number.

Passover, the "Season of Our Freedom," was so sacred to the Israelites that they were commanded to begin their calendar with the month in which this festival fell. But *Nisan* (as it is now called) was only the beginning of the *months*, not the beginning of the *year*. *Tishri*, the seventh month, marks the beginning of the new year. In the Torah, however, there is no mention of *Rosh Hashanah* as the "New Year."

The other months are not referred to by name in the Five Books of Moses. Not until we reach the books of Zekhariah, Esther, and Nehemiah are specific months mentioned. By that time the present names of the months had already come into being.*

There is no mention, either, in the Five Books of Moses of the number of days in each month.

Similar to that of the civil calendar, the Jewish week consists of seven days, which is evident from the first chapter of Genesis. Each month contains four weeks, plus one or two days, depending on the length of the month.

THE JEWISH DAY

The Jewish day, also as in the civil calendar, is twenty-four hours in length, but it begins at *sundown* instead of at midnight (as in the civil calendar). The days of the week (other than Sabbath, the seventh day) have no special names (as they do in the civil calendar) but are referred to by number. Thus, Sunday is the first day, Monday, the second day, and so forth.

No doubt the reason for this custom is because they all point in the direction of the Sabbath, which the observant Jew awaits anxiously from day to day. In other words, the first six days of the week have no intrinsic meaning in themselves; each one merely represents another number indicating our closeness to the Sabbath. Friday, however, is commonly called *Erev Shabbos*, since this is the day on which we prepare for the Sabbath.

As stated before, the day in Jewish tradition begins at sundown. In the Book of Genesis, God is said to have first created evening and then morning (Genesis 1:5).

---

*In the Book of Kings a few months are mentioned, but these names are entirely different from those of our present months. No further mention of them is found anywhere. See I Kings 8:2, 6:1, 37, 38.

Kislev   (29 or 30 days)

Teveth   (29 days)

SUMMARY

From the foregoing it will be clear to you that our Hebrew calendar is a combined solar and lunar calendar. Thus, even though the number of days in a year is lunar (354), the number of hours in a day (24) is solar. Also, during a leap year we add an extra month in order to adjust that year to the solar calendar, and to ensure that our festivals occur in their proper season.

In many other ways has this same calendar served us so faithfully and reliably for the past sixteen hundred years. Let us try to trace its growth and development, in order to come away with a clearer understanding of why it has been so invaluable to our people.

THE "WHY" OF OUR HEBREW CALENDAR
Its Background

Years ago, when most Jews were living together with their fellow Jews and had little contact with the outside, non-Jewish community, the Hebrew calendar was the only one in use. Thus, for birthdays, anniversaries, and other occasions we went by the Hebrew date only.

As the Jewish community began to mingle with the non-Jewish world, however, it became necessary to use both the civil and the Hebrew dates. That is why it is worthwhile to compare the civil calendar with our own, so that we can make use of both to our best advantage. (For this purpose, refer to the chart entitled "The Hebrew and Civil Calendars at a Glance.")

The Civil Calendar

The civil, or Gregorian, calendar now in common use was first established in its present form in 1582 by Pope Gregory XIII, after whom it was named.

It is a solar calendar because it is based on the movements of the earth around the sun, which, as we have already seen, are 365¼ days in length, with the day beginning at midnight. An extra day is added once every four years — on February 29 — as a result of the accumulation of an extra quarter day each year.

The years are counted from the birth of Jesus. We call this a "civil" calendar because it is the one most commonly used by the majority of people today. However, whenever we Jews refer to a date in this calendar, we do not call it by the Christian term "A.D." (Latin: *Anno Domini*, for "in the year of our Lord"), but rather "C.E.," "the Common Era." Thus, we speak of the year 1979 as 1979 C.E.

Shevat   (30 days)

Adar   (29 days)
      (in leap year 30)

The years before the year one of the civil calendar are referred to by us Jews as B.C.E., "Before the Common Era." Thus, the First Temple was destroyed in the year 586 B.C.E., or approximately, 2,566 years ago (1980 plus 586). B.C.E. is used instead of B.C. (Before Christ).

The days of the week in the civil calendar are named after the sun (Sunday), the moon (Monday), and certain Roman and pagan deities.

How Did Our Present Hebrew Calendar Come Into Being?

During the earliest days of our people, our ancestors used to reckon time from both the sun and the moon. However, they eventually realized it would be more convenient to count their months and years from the movements of the moon, and therefore they adopted the lunar year (354 days). (It is because of this fact that a "moon" also came to be known as a "month.")

Then, when our ancestors settled in their own land, Israel, they found it necessary to determine the first day of each month in order to know the date of each festival, as described in the Bible.

In the Temple days the dates of the festivals were determined by observers sent out by the Sanhedrin (the highest court and law-making body in the land) to spend a few nights watching the movements of the moon. They would then report back to the Sanhedrin the exact date of the beginning of the new moon, which would determine whether the outgoing month had twenty-nine or thirty days.

A beacon would be lit on top of one hill, the observer on the next hill would see it and light his own beacon, and the message of the New Moon would be relayed throughout the countryside. As long as the population was still small, mostly rural and scattered, this arrangement sufficed.

But such a system of announcing the new moon later proved unsatisfactory for the following reasons:

1) With the growth of Israel's population, fire signals became too dangerous because homes were built closer together.

2) The Samaritans (a people living in Israel who became unfriendly to the Jews) would often try to confuse them by lighting fire signals at the wrong time.

It therefore became customary for the Sanhedrin to send messengers to different parts of the country (and even outside Israel) to announce the exact date of *Rosh Ḥodesh*, the first of the month. However, if these messengers were not able to reach very distant places in time, leaving the first day of the month in doubt, many Jews who lived far from the centers or outside Israel altogether began observing two days, instead of one, for *Rosh Ḥodesh*, and an extra day for the festivals occurring during that month.

For this same reason — because the first day of the month was in doubt — Jews today living outside Israel observe an additional day for most of the major festivals. Thus, we have eight (instead of seven) days of Passover, two days (instead of one) of *Shavuot*, and nine (instead of eight) days of the *Sukkot* festival. Even in Israel, *Rosh Hashanah* has always been kept for two days; and *Yom Kippur* is observed for one day everywhere due to the difficulty of fasting for more than one day.

HOW ROSH ḤODESH IS OBSERVED

The only two commandments mentioned in the Bible with regard to observing *Rosh Ḥodesh* were the announcement through the sounding of trumpets (Numbers 10:10) and the special Temple sacrifices (Numbers 28:11-15). However, from other references to the new moon in the Bible,* we have reason to believe that, despite the fact that the Bible does not prohibit work on *Rosh Ḥodesh*, as it does for all the major festivals, this day was nevertheless observed as a major festival in ancient times. According to those references, *Rosh Ḥodesh* used to be celebrated with special feasts and sacrifices (I Samuel 20:18-34), visits to the Prophet (II Kings 4:23), and possible others not mentioned.

But as time went on, most of these customs fell out of use, so that today *Rosh Ḥodesh* is hardly marked at all by any particular celebration other than the recitation of special prayers and Torah readings.

The coming of the new moon is announced in the synagogue on the Sabbath preceding it. A special prayer, *Birkhat ha-Ḥodesh*, or the blessing of the new moon, is recited. In this prayer we also mention the time of the *Molad* — the exact moment when the moon stands between the sun and the earth. (*Rosh Ḥodesh* begins about six or more hours after this.) There then follows the official announcement of the name of the new month and the day, or days, on which *Rosh Ḥodesh* falls during the coming week. In this part of the prayer we say, for example, "*Rosh Ḥodesh Nisan* will be (observed) on Monday and Tuesday." Or, if *Rosh Ḥodesh* is only for one day that month, we say, ". . . on Tuesday."

If the outgoing month ends on the twenty-ninth, we observe only one day of *Rosh Ḥodesh*: the first of the new month. But if the old month ends on the thirtieth, we observe two days of *Rosh Ḥodesh*: the

* I Samuel 20:18; II Kings 4:23; Hosea 2:13; Isaiah 1:13, 66:23.

thirtieth (last day of the previous month) is the first day of *Rosh Ḥodesh*, and the first day of the new month is the second day of *Rosh Ḥodesh*.* (The prayer for the new moon is not recited for the month of *Tishri*, since a new year is beginning.)

On *Rosh Ḥodesh* itself certain prayers *(Ya'aleh v'Yavo*, the Half *Hallel*, and the *Musaf* for *Rosh Ḥodesh)* are recited, and a special Torah portion (Numbers 29:11-15) is read.

For *Rosh Ḥodesh* (as for other festivals) additional customs and observances are adhered to by many Jews in different lands. Here are a few:

1) Fasting and the recitation of penitential prayers (just as for a fast day) on the day before *Rosh Ḥodesh*.

2) Refraining (by women) from sewing and from certain other work during *Rosh Ḥodesh*.

3) Wearing new clothes for the first time on *Rosh Ḥodesh*, just as for a major festival.

SANCTIFICATION OF THE NEW MOON
(Kiddush ha-Levanah)

Just as we thank God for food and other benefits by reciting a blessing, we do the same for the new moon. We have a special ceremony called the Sanctification of the Moon, or *Kiddush ha-Levanah*, which is recited on a Saturday night between the third and the sixteenth of the month, and for which a *minyan* must be present for the recital of Kaddish. Immediately following the evening services, while everyone is still dressed in Sabbath clothes, the congregation stands outside to watch the moon, if it is visible.

A few appropriate prayers and blessings are then uttered. During these prayers people greet one another with the familiar Hebrew words, *shalom aleikhem* ("peace be unto you") and are answered by *aleikhem shalom*. Some Jews even dance and sing at this time.

The *Kiddush ha-Levanah* for the month of *Av* takes place at the close of the Fast of *Av*, and, for the month of *Tishri*, it is said following *Yom Kippur*.

CONCLUSION

From the material presented above, we can better understand the important part *Rosh Ḥodesh* plays in the life of our people, despite its being a minor festival. For one thing, it helps us adjust ourselves to the date of each festival, as well as providing us with another occasion to celebrate, even though we do not stop work on that day. *Rosh Ḥodesh* reminds us that a month has passed, and gives us further opportunity to thank God as we look forward to the arrival of each consecutive month.

---

* It should be noted that the observance of two days of *Rosh Ḥodesh* takes place mostly during the months in which a festival occurs.

It is interesting to note that while in biblical times the observance of *Rosh Ḥodesh* was marked by festivities as would befit a major holiday, today *Rosh Ḥodesh* is observed with only the few special *mitzvot* associated with it.

In Israel, the United States, and elsewhere, there are often special *Rosh Ḥodesh* programs and assemblies held in the Jewish schools and other institutions.

Also, it has recently been suggested in Israel that *Rosh Ḥodesh* be declared an official holiday so that Israelis, who work a six-day week with only Saturdays off, might have more of an opportunity to enjoy certain forms of recreation which Jews are forbidden to engage in on the Sabbath.

Such a proposal, which would serve the double purpose of making the Israelis more aware of *Rosh Ḥodesh* as a festival and providing them with an additional day for rest and enjoyment, is well worth considering.

The mere fact that *Rosh Ḥodesh* brings in a new month enables it to inject fresh hope into our lives, just as *Shabbat* does by bringing in a new week and *Rosh Hashanah* a new year.

This hope is perhaps most clearly expressed in the monthly blessing of the new moon, in which we ask God to grant us personally "all the wishes of our hearts," as well as for redemption (full freedom) for all Jews everywhere.

In this short chapter we have tried to describe the workings of the Jewish calendar and its related festival of *Rosh Ḥodesh*. You now know how we Jews count our days, weeks, months, and years, as time passes by.

But for us Jews merely "counting" time is not enough. In fact, our rabbis tell us that our Torah pays little attention to exact time or to the precise order of events related in the Scriptures. Instead, it is more concerned with what we *do* during that time, than with the amount of time that has elapsed. In other words, we Jews don't just "count" time. Rather, we make time *count* and have meaning for us.

In this connection we should ask ourselves: "What have I done during my lifetime to make every moment count? What have I done to enrich my life with a more careful observance of the *mitzvot*, with the study of Torah, with improving relations with other people?"

Only in this way will the study of the Hebrew calendar have any lasting value for us, because, as we have already seen, every single unit of time is very much a part of Jewish life.

THE HEBREW AND CIVIL CALENDARS AT A GLANCE:

A COMPARISON

	CIVIL CALENDAR	HEBREW CALENDAR
1) Based on movements of the:	Sun (Solar)	Moon (Lunar)
2) Length of year: a) Regular b) Leap year	a) 365¼ days b) 366 days	a) 353, 354, or 355 days b) 383, 384, or 385 days
3) Leap year: a) How often does it occur? b) How long does it last?	a) Every 4 years b) One additional *day*	a) Every 2 or 3 years, or 7 times in 19 years b) One additional *month*
4) Number of months in a year:	12	12, but 13 in a leap year
5) Years are numbered beginning with:	Birth of Jesus	Creation of the world
6) Example of year	1979	5739
7) In which month does the new year begin?	January, the *1st* month	*Tishri*, the 7th month
8) How are the months named?	Jan., Feb., etc., after Roman and other pagan deities	a) In the Bible, not by names, but by numbers (except *Aviv*) b) Mostly, at present, by Babylonian names (*Nisan, Iyar*, etc.)
9) How are the days named?	Sunday, (sun), Monday, (moon), and by pagan deities	Only by number, except Sabbath
10) Number of days in a week:	7	7
11) When does each day begin?	At midnight	At sundown
12) Day of rest:	Sunday	Saturday (Sabbath)
13) Author of present calendar:	Pope Gregory XIII, 1582	Hillel II, 360 C.E.

SUMMARY OF THE JEWISH
FESTIVALS OF THE YEAR

Rosh Hashanah: This festival marks the beginning of the Jewish New Year and is observed on the first and second days of the month of *Tishri*. On *Rosh Hashanah* we pray that every person will be inscribed in the Book of Life for the coming year. Amidst much prayer, the *Shofar* (ram's horn) is sounded to herald the beginning of the Ten Days of Penitence and to proclaim God as the Master of the world.

Yom Kippur (Day of Atonement): This, the holiest day of the entire year, is the last of the Ten Days of Penitence, when the Book of Life is finally sealed on the tenth day of *Tishri*. Beginning with the *Kol Nidrei* service just before sunset, all Jews, young and old, assemble in the synagogue to ask God for forgiveness of their sins, and fast from evening to evening.

Sukkot (Tabernacles): During the first seven days of this joyous
festival we dwell in a *sukkah* (small hut) as a reminder of the frail
huts in which the Israelites dwelled during their desert wanderings, when God protected them. We also use the *Four Species*
(etrog, lulav, myrtle, and willow leaves) to suggest to us the fruit
of harvest of old and which, together, are considered a kind of
"sceptre of God" which we are permitted to wield during these
holy days. *Simḥat Torah,* the day on which we rejoice in com-
pleting the Torah reading, marks the close of the *Sukkot* festival.

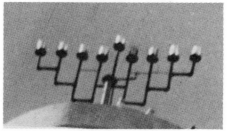

Hanukkah: The miracle of the oil in the Temple, which lasted for
eight days following the victory of the Maccabees over the
Syrians, is the reason why this festival is celebrated. To remind us
of this divine miracle, we light one new candle on each of the eight
nights of the festival.

Tu Bishvat (Fifteenth of *Sh'vat*): On this day tree-planting is
celebrated in Israel, which marks the beginning of the spring
season. In Israel it is observed as a gay festival; elsewhere, people
eat Israeli fruits and hold parties, celebrations, and the like.

160

Purim: It was on the fourteenth day of the month of *Adar* that the Jews of Persia were saved, through the efforts of Esther and Mordecai, from Haman's wicked plot to destroy them. This beautiful story is read in the *Megillah* (a small parchment scroll) on the evening and morning of *Purim*. The festival is a jolly one with much merrymaking and fun.

Pesaḥ (Passover): As the "Season of Our Freedom," we celebrate the liberation of our ancestors from Egyptian slavery during this eight-day festival by having a *Seder* on the first two nights. At this special home service we retell the story of the exodus from Egypt (as stated in the Bible) by means of certain symbols that are found on the festival table. We eat *matzot* instead of bread throughout the entire eight days, since all foods containing leaven are forbidden.

161

Lag b'Omer: It was on this day, the thirty-third day of the Counting of the Omer, that a plague that had killed off thousands of students of Rabbi Akiba (about 130 C.E.) suddenly stopped. It has therefore been observed as a day of joy ever since. All festivities usually forbidden during the days after Passover are permitted on *Lag b'Omer*.

Shavuot (Feast of Weeks): This two-day festival is observed for two reasons: to commemorate the giving of the Torah on Mount Sinai, and to remind us of the *bikkurim* (first-fruit's offerings) that were brought to the Temple as a thanksgiving offering of the early (grain) harvest. During this festival both the synagogue and the home are decorated with green branches.

162

Rosh Ḥodesh (New Moon): This half-holiday is observed at the beginning of every Hebrew month, as commanded in the Bible. During ancient times it was said to have been celebrated as a full holiday, even though Scripture does not forbid work on this day. Today, however, its observance is generally confined to the recitation of special prayers and Torah reading.

Yom Yerushalayim (Day of Jerusalem Reunited): Following nineteen years of Arab rule throughout the Old City (including the Western Wall), it finally became reunited with the rest of Jerusalem on the twenty-eighth day of *Iyar*, or, June 7, 1967, as a result of the Six-Day War. Its observance is still in formation.

Israeli Independence Day: We celebrate this day to mark Israel's having become an independent nation on the fifth of *Iyar* (May 14, 1948), after nearly two thousand years of foreign rule. This young festival is celebrated in Israel with many festivities and throughout the world in many other ways.

For a comprehensive treatment of the festivals, see Morris Golomb, *Know Your Festivals and Enjoy Them*, Shengold Publishers, New York, 1973.

HOW OUR CALENDAR IS ADJUSTED TO THE DATES OF THE FESTIVALS

Here are a few ways by means of which our Hebrew calendar is adjusted to the various festivals.

The first day of Rosh Hashanah can never fall on a *Sunday*, *Wednesday*, or *Friday*. Why not?

1) It cannot fall on a *Sunday* because that would make Hoshana Rabbah (the 7th day of Sukkot) fall on the Sabbath, when beating the willow leaves for "Hoshanot" is forbidden.

2) It cannot fall on a *Wednesday* because if if did, Yom Kippur would then fall on a Friday, when it would be impracticable to prepare for the Sabbath.

3) It cannot fall on a *Friday* for it would make Yom Kippur fall on a Sunday, which would also be impracticable, especially for the preparation of food.

So as to prevent Rosh Hashanah from falling at those times, an extra day is added to one year and then subtracted from the next.

Thus, whenever the extra day is added, an ordinary year contains 355 days and a leap year, 385 days, while a year with one day less has 353 days if it is an ordinary year or 383, if it is a leap year.

As a result, we have years of six different lengths, as follows:

353 days — a "short" regular year (when one day is substracted)
354 days — a complete regular year
355 days — a "full" regular year (when one day is added)
383 days — a "short" leap year
384 days — a regular leap year
385 days — a "full" leap year.

The extra day is always added to the month of *Heshvan* and subtracted from the month of *Kislev*.

CONCLUSION

Judaism is not just a weekend or a synagogue religion. It covers the whole of life. You practice your Judaism not only when you are performing a religious act, such as observing the Sabbath, praying three times daily, or eating a kosher meal, but even when you are playing a game, studying, watching TV, or relaxing. Whatever you do, you are the same person and that includes your being a Jew.

A Jew derives meaning and satisfaction for his life from his Judaism. He faces the future with hope because he realizes that, no matter what trials or sorrows he may go through, it will, in the end, turn out for the best because they are part of God's plan.

This optimistic outlook is expressed throughout the literature of Judaism. Already in the story of the Creation we learn that God looked at everything He had made "and, behold, it was very good" (Genesis 1:31).

Throughout its long history, the Jewish people have seen untold persecution and suffering. But its belief in the ultimate redemption has always remained strong. During the dark days of the Nazi Holocaust, Jews on their way to the gas chambers sang and danced, determined to express their complete faith in God no matter what the reality that confronted them. Such instances of rejoicing in the midst of suffering are also to be found during other periods of our history.

When the Jew practices the various customs and ceremonies described in this book, he does so willingly and joyfully, not only because he finds pleasure in observing them but also because of his love for God Whose commands they represent. Yet another vital source of delight for the Jew has been study and knowledge. As a matter of fact, every Jew is required to set aside a definite time for study each day as part of his daily routine.

The material in this book has provided some basic information about how enjoyable Jewish life can be. The explanations for many of the observances described have offered you an additional source of knowledge. However, since this book could not go deeply into every area of Jewish living, it is to be hoped that you will seek to add to your knowledge by further reading. A good starting point for your additional reading would be the Biblical references that have been given in connection with the various topics discussed. This in turn should provide a foundation for further study.

By broadening the scope of your Jewish learning, you will find that your day-to-day observance of the various mitzvoth will become much more meaningful and will add to your sense of Jewish identity.

It is my sincere hope that you will live a full life as a Jew and enjoy every moment of it.

אֵין מְבִיאִין בִּכּוּרִים חוּץ מִשִּׁבְעַת הַמִּינִים

QUIZ QUESTIONS
AND
ANSWERS

BIRTH, CIRCUMCISION AND EARLY CHILDHOOD CEREMONIES IN JEWISH LIFE

QUESTIONS

1. What makes a person Jewish?

2. Name the first cermony required to be performed for a new-born Jewish boy.

3. When and where is an infant girl usually named?

4. Give the exact meaning of the term "Brit Milah."

5. a) With whom did God first make the "Covenant of Circumcision"?
   b) How did Abraham fulfill the duty of this Covenant?

6. a) What is a circumcision?
   b) When is it performed?

7. Can a *Brit Milah* ever be postponed?

8. A circumcision is a sign of _____.

9. During which two periods of Jewish history was circumcision forbidden?

ANSWERS

1. He is born of a Jewish mother or has been properly converted to Judaism.

2. Circumcision.

3. On the first opportunity following her birth, in the synagogue, when her father is called to the Torah.

4. The Covenant of Circumcision.

5. a) With Abraham and his descendants. (See Genesis 17:9-12).
   b) By circumcising first himself and then his sons and his male servants.

6. a) A minor operation performed on a male child.
   b) On the eighth day after birth.

7. Yes, if the infant is ill or too weak for the procedure.

8. God's Covenant with Abraham.

9. During the Maccabean period (about 168 B.C.E.) and during the second war with Rome (about 130 C.E.). Circumcision was made subject to the death penalty, but mothers, together with their sons, gave up their

10. Complete the following sentence:
During Biblical times a Jew had to be circumcised in order to be permitted to _____.

11. How do our sages feel about the importance of *Brit Milah*?

12. a) What is a "Shalom Zachor" celebration?
b) When is it observed?

13. Name a few ways in which this event is celebrated.

14. a) Why do we Jews observe circumcision?
b) Why do some non-Jews practice it?

15. Can a *Brit Milah* be held on a Sabbath or festival?

16. During what part of the day is a circumcision usually performed? Why?

17. In ancient times who would usually perform a circumcision?

18. Who is permitted to perform a circumcision?

lives rather than let their children remain uncircumcised.

10. Offer the Paschal lamb on Passover.

11. It is equal in importance to all the other commandments of our Torah.

12. a) It is a "welcome to the male child."
b) It is observed on the Friday night before the *Brit Milah*. The literal meaning of "Shalom" is peace. It expresses the hope that the new-born baby will bring peace to the world.

13. Usually as a party given at the home. It includes songs and prayers for the welfare of the child.

14. a) As a sign of the Covenant between God and Abraham.
b) As an "initiation rite," and also as a hygienic measure. Moslems perform it at the age of 12 or 13; other societies, just before marriage.

15. Yes. It must be held on the eighth day after birth, even if that day should fall on Yom Kippur.

16. During the forenoon, in remembrance of how Abraham had arisen early in order to fulfill God's command.

17. The father.

18. A *mohel* — an observant Jew

172

19. Name two other persons (besides the father and the mohel) who take part in the circumcision ceremony.

20. What is the "Chair of Elijah"? What does it symbolize?

21. a) When is the male child named?
    b) Why only then?

22. After whom is a child usually named?

23. a) If an infant boy is named Joseph, and his father's name is Abraham, how is his named stated in Hebrew?
    b) How is the name of a girl, named Sarah, expressed in Hebrew, if her parents' names are David and Leah?

24. Give the meaning of the term "Pidyon ha-Ben."

25. Later, the duty to enter the active service of the Lord passed from the first-born sons to the Levites. Why?

who is an expert in the procedure and the laws of circumcision.

19. a) The *sandek*, or godfather, who holds the child during the ceremony.
    b) The *qwatter, or the* person who hands the child to the *mohel.*

20. A special chair set aside during a circumcision ceremony for the Prophet Elijah, who is regarded as the guardian of newborn children and the messenger of peace and deliverance.

21. a) Immediately following the circumcision.
    b) It was after his circumcision that Abraham's name was changed from Abram to Abraham (Genesis 17:5).

22. After a departed relative. Sephardic families usually name children after living relatives.

23. a) Joseph *ben* Abraham (Joseph son of Abraham).
    b) Sarah *bat* David (Sarah, daughter of David).

24. Redemption of the firstborn son. The ceremony has its origins in Exodus 13:13 and Numbers 18:16. It was originally instituted to "redeem" the first-born son from his obligation to enter the service of the Lord.

25. Because the Levites were the only ones not to participate in the worship of the Golden Calf in the wilderness (Exodus 32).

26. On which day after birth is a *Pidyon ha-Ben* ceremony to be observed?

26. On the 31st day after birth.

27. During the *Pidyon ha-Ben* ceremony the a)_____ buys back the b)_____ from the c)_____ for a sum of d)_____.

27. a) Father.
    b) Son.
    c) Kohen.
    d) The equivalent of five shekels.

28. a) Who is required to have a *Pidyon ha-Ben?*
    b) Who is not required to have one?

28. a) A first-born male, naturally-born, who is the son of a Jewish mother.
    b) The son of a Kohen or a Levite, or the son of a daughter of a Kohen or a Levite.

29. a) What is the only reason for which the *Pidyon ha-Ben* can be postponed?
    b) What if the circumcision has not yet been held?

29. a) If the 31st day falls on a Sabbath or a festival.
    b) A *Pidyon ha-Ben* still may not be postponed.

30. During the conversation between the father and the Kohen, what is the question asked, and of whom? What is the answer?

30. The Kohen asks the father whether he wants to give him the child, or whether he wants to "redeem" him. The father then says that he wants to "redeem" the boy.

31. a) What is a first-born male child required to do after he grows up?
    b) How can he be released from this fast?

31. a) Fast every *Erev Pesah*, as a reminder of how the first born males of the Egyptians were killed, but those of the Jews were saved (Exodus 11).
    b) By attending a *Siyyum ha-Torah*.

32. What is a *Siyyum ha-Torah?*

32. A celebration held when the study of a holy book is completed.

JEWISH EDUCATION

1. Why doesn't learning ever end for a Jew?

1. Because Jewish literature is so vast that no one can claim to be able to study all of it even during a lifetime.

2. Name some great Jewish scholars from ancient times who had to struggle to study the Torah.

2. Hillel, who could not afford tuition fees and almost froze to death lying on the roof of the house of study in the winter to listen to the lectures; and Rabbi Akiva, who started out as an ignorant shepherd and left his wife while he went to study Torah.

3. What is meant by "Tanakh"?

3. This is the Hebrew term for the Bible. It is composed of the initial letters for the words, "Torah" (Law); "Neviim" (Prophets); and "Ketubim" (Holy Writings).

4. a) What is the "Oral Law"?
   b) Name its two parts.

4. a) The Oral Tradition that explain the Biblical Law.
   b) Mishnah and Gemara.

5. True or false: Among the Jews only the brightest children were ever given an education.

5. False. It was considered obligatory for every Jewish child, whether or not he was bright, to study the lore of Judaism.

6. Name at least two basic religious Jewish subjects which a Jew should study.

6. Bible (Torah); Talmud; Shulhan Arukh (code of Jewish Law).

7. Name three or more secular (non-religious) subjects which are helpful in acquiring a good knowledge of Judaism.

7. Hebrew language; Jewish history; Zionism.

8. What is the most desirable time to begin your Jewish education?

8. Before the age of five — the earlier the better.

9. If you never attended Hebrew school, is it too late for you to acquire a Jewish education?

9. No. You can enroll at adult classes given at synagogues and other Jewish institutions, attend lectures on Jewish topics, and read Jewish books and periodicals.

BAR MITZVAH

1. You are not considered to be Bar Mitzvah unless you:
   a) Have a special Bar Mitzvah ceremony.
   b) Gain a certain amount of Jewish knowledge.
   c) Have reached the age of 13 years and 1 day.

1. c) Have reached the age of 13 years and 1 day.

2. What is the significance of the Bar Mitzvah ceremony?

2. It celebrates your having "come of age" as regards religious observance, and gives you a chance to show your friends and relatives that you have acquired a certain amount of Jewish knowledge.

3. Which of the following things does not belong at a Sabbath Bar Mitzvah ceremony?
   Reciting a *Haftorah*; wearing a *tallit*; reciting a number of blessings; wearing *tefillin*.

3. Wearing *tefillin*, because *tefillin* must not be worn on the Sabbath.

4. What is the *trop*?

4. The traditional chant used in the reading of the books of the Bible.

5. How many Jewish male adults are called up for an *Aliyah* (Torah honor) on a Sabbath?

5. Seven.

6. Number the following in their correct order of the Sabbath or festival service:
   Musaf service; *Shaharit* service; *Haftorah*; Torah reading; removing the Torah from the Ark.

6. 1) *Shaharit*; 2) removing Torah; 3) Torah reading; 4) *Haftorah*; 5) *Musaf* service.

7. Name two or more things you are expected to do following Bar Mitzvah.

7. a) Continue your Jewish studies.
   b) Wear *tallit* and *tefillin* regularly, as well as observing other mitzvot.
   c) Make use of your new rights and privileges as a Jewish adult.

8. Does Bar Mitzvah imply that you have completed your Jewish studies?

9. What are some of the rights and privileges which you gain when you become Bar Mitzvah?

8. No. A good Jew keeps on studying Jewish law and literature throughout his life.

9. a) The right to become part of a *minyan*.

b) The privilege of being given an *Aliyah* whenever the Torah is read.

c) The right to lead the services as cantor.

d) If you are a Kohen, the privilege of blessing the congregation during the "Dukhan" service on festivals.

e) The right to serve as a witness in a court of Jewish law.

f) (The obligation) to wear *tallit* and *tefillin* regularly.

TALLIT AND TEFILLIN

QUESTIONS

1. A Jew's "uniform" consists of his ____ and ____.

2. The Hebrew word "tzitzit" means _____.

3. What makes the *tallit* a holy garment?

4. a) What is a "tallit katan"?
   b) When must it be worn?

5. When is the *tallit* worn?

6. Of how many parts do the *tefillin* consist?

ANSWERS

1. *Tallit* and *tefillin*.

2. Fringes.

3. The *tzitzit*, or fringes, which the Bible (Num. 15:37-41) commands males to wear so that they may be reminded of God's commandments.

4. a) It is a four-cornered piece of linen or cloth with the fringes on its four corners and an opening in the center large enough to admit the head.

   b) It is worn by males throughout the day.

5. During the prayer services.

6. Of two parts: one for the head *(shel rosh)* and one for the left arm *(shel yad).*

7. What is contained inside each part of the *tefillin?*

7. Parchment on which are written four passages from Exodus 13:1-10; 11-16; Deut. 6:4-9; 11:13-21.

8. How does the arrangement of the text on the parchment in the *shel yad* differ from that of the *shel rosh?*

8. In the *shel rosh* each passage is written on a separate piece of parchment, while in the *shel yad* all four passages are written on one single piece of parchment.

9. Why have we been commanded to wear the *tallit* and *tefillin?*

9. So that they may serve us as physical reminders of the mitzvot of the Torah.

10. Why don't women wear *tallit* and *tefillin?*

10. Because a woman is not required to observe commandments dependent on any specific time of day.

11. To what does the following quotation refer?
"And you shall bind them for a sign . . . and they shall be for frontlets . . ." (Deut. 6:8).

11. *Tefillin.*

12. What meaning does the wearing of *tefillin* have for a Bar Mitzvah boy?

12. It shows that he has now become an adult as regards his obligation to observe the laws of Judaism.

13. a) When do men put on the *tefillin?*
b) When are they not to be worn?
c) Give reasons for a and b.

13. a) On weekdays only.
b) On Sabbath and festivals.
c) Since the Sabbaths and festivals are themselves a "sign" of God's Covenant with Israel, the tefillin become unnecessary as a "sign" on these days.

14. Name the one day in the year when *tefillin* are not worn at the regular time. Why?

14. The morning of the fast of the Ninth of *Av.* Tefillin are regarded as a spiritual ornament which we feel should not be worn on a day of mourning.

15. a) Which Hebrew word is formed from the two sections of the *tefillin?*
b) How is the word formed?

15. a) *Shad-dai* (God Almighty).
b) The letter *shin* formed from the *shel yad;* the *dalet* from the knot on the *shel rosh;* and the *yod* from the knot on the *shel yad.*

16. Give the order to be followed when removing the
tefillin.

17. How must the *tefillin* be
cared for?

18. When must the *tallit* and
tefillin be put on in the
morning?

19. Give at least two symbolic
values to be gained from
wearing *tallit* and *tefillin*.

20. Why do Jewish males wear a
head covering?

21. Does the *yarmulka* or *kippah* in itself have any
religious significance?

22. Which is put on first, the
tallit or the *tefillin*? Why?

16. *The shin* formed on the
hand is removed first, the
shel rosh next, followed by
the *shel yad*.

17. They must be checked every
few years by a *sofer*
(Hebrew Scribe) to be sure
that the parchment, writing,
and all other parts are still in
good condition.

18. Before breakfast.

19. a) It symbolizes your Jewish
identity.
b) It reminds you of your
obligation to observe the
Divine commandments.
c) It implies that Jewish
observance demands not
only thought but also ac-
tion.

20. As a sign of reverence to
God. It is considered disrespectful to appear in
God's presence with one's
head uncovered.

21. No; it simply serves as a
handy, comfortable head
covering.

22. The *tallit*, because it is worn
every day, while the *tefillin*
are worn on weekdays only.

THE SYNAGOGUE IN JEWISH LIFE

QUESTIONS

1. Give the basic definition of
a synagogue.

2. What are the three Hebrew
names given to a syn-
agogue?

ANSWERS

1. The synagogue is a place set
aside for prayer.

2. a) *Bet Tefillah* — House of
Prayer.
b) *Bet ha-Midrash* — House
of Study.
c) *Bet ha-Knesset* — House

3. Choose the correct answer in parentheses:
A synagogue is necessary for (formal, informal) prayer.

4. When did synagogues as we know them today first come into existence?

5. Number, in their correct chronological order, the following places of worship before there was a synagogue: Temple, Altars, Sanctuary.

6. Which two basic prayers, still used today, were recited also in the earliest synagogues?

7. When were most of the synagogue services we know today first instituted?

8. Why has the synagogue been called a "mikdash me'at" ("small sanctuary")?

9. Which two holy objects would you find in any synagogue, and why?

10. Name the three major branches of American Judaism.

11. a) What is a "Meḥitzah"?
b) In which type of synagogue is it usually found?
c) Give at least one reason for its use.

12. Name one practice (other than prayer) that is observed in every syn-

---

of Assembly (for worship and for other purposes).

3. Formal prayer.

4. About 586 B.C.E. after the destruction of the First Temple.

5. Altars, Sanctuary, Temple.

6. The *Shema* and the *Amidah*.

7. In the Talmudic period.

8. Because it took the place of the Temple as a place of worship after the Temple had been destroyed.

9. The Holy Ark and a *Ner Tamid* ("Eternal Light"). Both of these were also part of the Temple.

10. Orthodox, Conservative, Reform.

11. a) A partition which separates the men's and women's sections.
b) Orthodox.
c) The Temple in Jerusalem had an *Ezrat Nashim* or women's section. Men and women can concentrate on their prayers more effectively when seated separately.

12. Reading the Torah at least once a week.

agogue, Orthodox, Conservative or Reform.

13. Why must the Torah be read on at least three different days each week?

13. So that no three days will ever go by without the Torah being read at least once.

14. Give three examples of how a synagogue fulfills its function as a *Bet ha-Midrash* (House of Study).

14. Rabbi's sermons, adult classes, public lectures, Hebrew and/or Sunday School, Hebrew Day School or *Yeshivah*.

15. What kind of functions does a synagogue conduct when it serves as a *Bet ha-Knesset* (House of Assembly)?

15. Bar Mitzvah or wedding celebrations, *Kiddush* following services, meetings for various organizations.

16. How does the work of a modern rabbi differ from that of rabbis in earlier days?

16. The rabbi today often serves not only as a preacher and teacher but also as a friend and guide to his congregants and as a leader in communal activities.

17. What is meant by "semikhah"?

17. Ordination, or, being certified by a recognized institution or outstanding authority as possessing the Torah knowledge required of a rabbi.

18. Name a few qualities, in addition to having a pleasing voice, which a cantor must possess.

18. Knowledge of prayers and traditional melodies; good character and piety.

19. What are a few of the duties of a *shammash* (sexton)?

19. Supervise daily services; care for the religious articles of the synagogue; assist in any other way that he can around the synagogue.

20. How many people are required for organizing a congregation?

20. At least ten adult males (a *minyan*).

21. Must everyone praying in a synagogue be a member of the congregation?

21. Not necessarily, but as a rule regular worshippers at any one synagogue become members of the congregation in order to help maintain the synagogue and its institutions.

22. If you are unable to attend synagogue service, may you recite your prayers at home?

22. Yes, except for those prayers which can be recited only with a *minyan*.

23. Name a few things that are forbidden in a synagogue.

23. a) Eating or drinking.
b) Running about.
c) Whispering, conversing, or distrubing the service in any other way.

24. Why is a *minyan* required for a synagogue service?

24. Because certain prayers cannot be recited, and the Torah reading cannot be conducted, unless a *minyan* is present.

MARRIAGE AND DIVORCE IN JUDAISM

MARRIAGE

QUESTIONS

ANSWERS

1. What are usual steps to be followed for a Jewish marriage?

1. a) Both members must be Jewish.
b) The engagement.
c) The traditional wedding ceremony.
d) Fulfilling the necessary requirements of the civil law.

2. Name at least one danger of intermarriage.

2. a) It weakens the attachment of our whole people to Judaism.
b) If the woman is the non-Jewish partner, the children born of that marriage are not Jewish.

3. Correct the following sentence:
A Jewish couple may be married either under civil or Jewish law.

3. A Jewish marriage must be conducted under both Jewish law and civil law.

4. Why is a wedding forbidden to be held on a Sabbath or holidays?

4. Because a wedding is a form of contract, and no business may be transacted during a Sabbath or festival.

182

5. What is meant by the "aufruf"?

6. Name the objects and other requirements for a Jewish wedding ceremony.

7. What is the purpose of the ring?

8. What is the "ketubah"?

9. a) Name the 2 basic parts of a Jewish wedding.
   b) What act is performed by both the bride and the groom following each part?

10. What is meant by the "Seven Marriage Blessings"?

11. What is the significance of breaking a glass at the close of the wedding ceremony?

12. a) Which of the following terms does not belong there? Ḥuppah, two witnesses, aufruf, yihud, seven blessings, veiling the bride.
    b) Why not?

13. What reasons are given for the following?
    a) Fasting on the wedding day.
    b) Yihud.

5. The custom of the groom being called to the Torah shortly before his wedding day.

6. Ḥuppah, wine, ketubah, ring, two witnesses, and, if possible, a minyan.

7. To show that the groom is giving his bride some article of value.

8. The marraige contract which sets forth the agreement between the bride and groom.

9. a) The "Betrothal" and the final act of marriage.
   b) Each one drinks from a cup of wine.

10. Those seven that are usually chanted or recited by the rabbi, cantor, or guest rabbis following the reading of the ketubah and also during the week following the wedding ceremony.

11. One explanation is as a reminder of the destruction of the Temple — something we must never forget, even amidst our greatest joy.

12. a) Aufruf.
    b) It is not a part of the wedding ceremony.

13. a) So that bride and groom may begin their married life atoned, and free from sin.
    b) To give the couple their first opportunity to be together as husband and wife.

QUESTIONS   ANSWERS

1. By whom may a divorce proceeding be conducted?
2. Why is a *sofer* (scribe) necessary for a divorce to be granted?
3. a) To whom and by whom must a *get* be delivered?
   b) In case of any problem in delivering the *get*, who usually does it?
4. What information is included in a *get*?

5. Name one restriction to be observed in a remarriage following a divorce.

1. A *bet din*, or Jewish Court.
2. He must write the bill of divorce.
3. a) To the wife by the husband.
   b) A *shaliah*, or messenger.
4. Full names of both parties; Hebrew and civil dates; name of city and state where *get* was written.
5. A divorced woman may not marry a *Kohen*."

KASHRUT: YOU ARE WHAT YOU EAT

QUESTIONS   ANSWERS

1. Define each of the following:
   a) kosher
   b) *kashrut*
   c) dietary laws
2. a) To what does the term "kosher" refer, besides food?
   b) Give a few examples.

3. Why is kashrut so important to the Jew?

4. Name the three basic pillars upon which the Jewish religion rests.
5. About how many of the 613

1. a) That which is fit, proper, or permitted by Jewish law.
   b) The state of being kosher.
   c) Laws that deal with kosher food.
2. a) See 1a above.
   b) A synagogue, Torah scroll, *tallit*, *etrog*, *lulav*, *mezuzah*, and even a person's conduct.
3. It is one of the pillars upon which Judaism rests. Also, it has been said that a person's eating habits affect his conduct.
4. *Kashrut*, Sabbath, and Family Purity.
5. 50.

commandments of the
Torah deal with *kashrut*?

6. Where are the laws of
kashrut explained?

7. Give the two terms which
mean the opposite of
"kosher."

8. According to the Bible, what
three things do the com-
mandments of *kashrut* do
for us?

9. Does the Torah mention
health as a reason regarding
kashrut?

10. How many of the seven
steps that make meat kosher
can you name (briefly)?

11. What two qualifications
must a four-legged animal
have in order to be permitted as food under the dietary
laws?

6. The Bible and Talmud.

7. *Trafe, Pasul.*

8. a) They make us holy before
God.
b) They enable us to tell the
difference between clean
and unclean foods.
c) They separate us from
other peoples who do not
observe the laws of *kashrut*.

9. No.

10. a) The animal must not be
among the animals forbid-
den by Biblical law.
b) The animal must be
properly slaughtered by a
qualified *shohet*.
c) The *shohet* must examine
the meat and find it free of
disease or other defect.
d) The blood must be
drained by soaking and
salting.
e) The meat must be
prepared in kosher utensils.
f) The meat must be kept
away from dairy foods and
anything non-kosher.
g) The entire process must
be under strict *kashrut*
supervision.

11. It must chew its cud and
have a split hoof. If the
animal has only one of these
two qualifications it is not
kosher.

12. A "clean" animal is first mentioned in the Bible in connection with whom?
a) Adam; b) Noah; c) Abraham; d) Moses

13. The permitted animals tend to eat what foods?

14. Fill in the blanks:
An animal whose hoof is not split may often use his hoof as a ____ in order to do ____ to other living things.

15. What is a *shohet*?

16. What is a fundamental principle which guides the *shohet* in the act of slaughtering?

17. Why must a slaughtered animal's carcass be carefully examined following slaughter?

18. In which sources are the laws regarding ritual slaughter of animals found?

19. Why is it considered such a serious sin for Jews to eat blood?

20. In what ways is the blood of an animal drained?

21. Upon which Biblical verse are the laws separating meat and dairy foods based?

22. What is the difference between steps 1,2,3,4, and 5,6,7?

23. a) Why are separate dishes and other utensils for meat and dairy foods necessary?
b) What else besides the dishes must be kept separate?

12. b) Noah.

13. Vegetation.

14. Weapon, harm.

15. A slaughterer of kosher meat.

16. That the animal should suffer as little pain as possible. This should teach us to be kind to all living things.

17. To look for any signs of infection, disease, injury, etc.

18. In the Talmud (Tractate *Hulin*) and in *Yoreh Deah*, a section of the *Shulhan Arukh*.

19. Because blood symbolizes the life of a living thing; hence, eating blood is like consuming the very life of the animal.

20. It is soaked and then salted. Liver must be broiled over an open fire.

21. "Thou shalt not boil a kid in its mother's milk."

22. Steps 1-4 tell us how meat becomes kosher, while steps 5, 6, and 7 show us how it can remain kosher.

23. a) To make sure that the two types of food are not mixed.
b) Pots and pans, cutlery, utensils or anything else coming in contact with the food.

24. a) In order to be effective, *kashrut* must be observed (choose):
Part of the way/Most of the way/All of the way.
b) What is the danger in violating steps 5 and 6 even though the first four have been obeyed?

25. When we open an egg, we must examine it carefully for what?

26. If meat is not kashered within 72 hours after slaughter, what must be done to it?

27. What is a *Va'ad ha-Kashrut?*

28. What is a *mashgiah?* What are his duties?

29. Of what value is the *Va'ad ha-Kashrut?*

30. What qualifications must a *shohet* meet?

31. What requirements must a Jewish meat market meet in order to be considered kosher?

24. a) All of the way.
b) The meat can become as *trafe* as if the first four steps had never been followed.

25. To make sure that it does not show a blood spot. A blood spot makes the egg unfit for use.

26. It must be washed in cool water within 72 hours.

27. An organization that supervises *kashrut* in a Jewish community.

28. A person who is personally present in a slaughterhouse, butcher shop, restaurant or hotel to make sure that these places observe the dietary laws properly.

29. It is there to assure you of getting strictly kosher meat.

30. a) He must personally be an observant Jew.
b) He must be learned in Jewish law, particularly the laws regarding ritual slaughter and ritual examination of animals.
c) He must be skilled in the act of slaughtering.

31. a) Only kosher meat is sold there.
b) It is closed on Sabbaths and Jewish holidays.
c) The butcher personally is an observant Jew.
d) The butcher knows how to take care of the meat.
e) It has proper rabbinic supervision.

32. For how long must the meat be soaked in water? Salted?

33. What is the purpose of soaking and salting the meat?

34. How is an animal or fowl marked to indicate proper slaughtering and inspection?

35. Are there differences between the slaughtering laws regarding quadrupeds and fowls?

36. What two requirements must fish meet in order to be kosher?

37. Give a few example of kosher and non-kosher fish.

38. Why is it forbidden to dip a fowl in hot water in order to remove the feathers before kashering it?

39. Define *ḥametz*.

40. Where are we commanded not to eat *ḥametz* during Passover?

41. Why are we forbidden to eat *ḥametz* during Passover?

42. What is a *Mezumen*?

43. How do you express your thanks to God for the food you have eaten?

44. Name one way of identifying a kosher product.

---

32. Soaked for half an hour and salted for one hour.

33. To remove *all* the blood.

34. For animals, it is marked by a special stamped label. For fowls, a *plumba* (lead tag) is attached.

35. Yes, but very few, because the basic laws of *kashrut* apply to both quadrupeds and fowls.

36. They must have both fins and scales.

37. Kosher: pike, halibut, mackerel, trout, salmon. Non-kosher: shellfish, oysters, clams, lobsters, crabs.

38. This can interfere with draining the blood, and cause other problems.

39. Food forbidden to be used during Passover because it is or contains leaven.

40. In the Bible.

41. To recall that the Children of Israel had to leave Egypt so suddenly that they could not wait for their dough to rise and turn into bread.

42. The smallest number (three) of adult men who can recite the Grace after Meals as a group.

43. By saying the Grace after Meals or, if it was just a snack, by reciting a shorter blessing after you eat.

44. If it bears a special label such as the Ⓤ and others.

45. Which is the most reliable way of determining whether a product is actually kosher?

45. Finding out if the rabbi who has approved the product is reliable.

46. What, besides your food, must always be kosher in your daily life?

46. Everything that is used in observing your Judaism, such as a synagogue, a Torah, a *tallit*, *tefillin*, a mezuzah, etc., and all of your thoughts, actions, and deeds, both those involving yourself, and those involving others.

THE HOME IN JEWISH LIFE

QUESTIONS

1. What is the first outward sign that tells you that a home is Jewish?

2. What makes a *mezuzah* a holy object?

3. Which rooms in the house, in addition to the main entrance, require a *mezuzah*?

4. May a *mezuzah* be worn on the body as a personal ornament?

5. What is "Ḥanukat ha-Bayit"?

6. Name some of the important ceremonies or customs that take place during a Ḥanukat ha-Bayit.

ANSWERS

1. A *mezuzah* on the door.

2. The fact that the roll of parchment inside the case contains passages from the Bible (Deuteronomy 6:4-9; 11:13-21).

3. All rooms except the bathroom.

4. No. If you wish, you can wear the outer case, but the parchment scroll must be removed first.

5. A house-warming ceremony held when moving into a new home.

6. a) Affixing the *mezuzah* to the doorpost with the proper blessing.
b) Special prayers found in some prayer books.
c) Bringing bread and salt into the new home.

7. Why is a *mezuzah* attached to a Jewish home?

7. a) Because of the commandment in Deuteronomy 6:9: "And thou shalt write them [i.e., the words of God] upon the doorposts of thy house and on thy gates."
b) To identify your home as being Jewish.

8. Name some religious objects that are often found in a Jewish home.

8. Sabbath candlesticks, the eight-branched *Ḥanukkah* menorah, spice box for the *Havdalah* ceremony, *tallit* and *tefillin*, *ḥallah* and *matzo* covers.

9. What arrangement would you expect to find in a traditional Jewish kitchen?

9. Two sets of dishes and kosher food.

10. Why does the Fifth Commandment tell us to "honor" our parents instead of simply "obeying" them?

10. Because "honoring" includes not only obeying one's parents but also showing them respect and love.

11. How did the observance of Jewish traditions help the Jews survive as a people although they were living among non-Jews?

11. The observance of Jewish traditions helped strengthen their morale and their family life.

12. Can you name some qualities found in the ideal Jewish home?

12. Harmony, love, contentment, and a sense of Jewish identity fostered by religious observance.

13. The literal meaning of the word "Tzedakah" is:
a) Charity
b) Pity
c) Righteousness

13. c) Righteousness. Judaism considers charity as an act of righteousness toward the poor.

14. What is meant by *Shalom Bayit?*

14. Harmony in the home. This is one of the qualities for which the Jewish home is best known among non-Jews.

15. Name a few ways in which you can help achieve *Shalom Bayit.*

15. a) Respect your parents and elders.
b) Observe the Sabbath and festivals.

16. How do the festivals help create a good Jewish atmosphere in the Jewish home?
17. What is the place of children in religious observance?

18. What is the best way of encouraging others to practice Jewish observances?

19. What steps are suggested to help keep a Jewish home observant?

16. By bringing all the members of the family together in worthwhile and spiritually uplifting activities.
17. Observances centering around children include *B'rit Milah*, *Pidyon ha-Ben* and Bar Mitzvah. In addition, many other observances, such as the Sabbath and festivals, focus greatly on children.
18. Observe your Judaism in your own life and show by your own personal example how such observances can improve the quality of life.
19. a) Knowing and understanding the reasons for many of these observances.
b) Willingness to make sacrifices for such observances as Sabbath and dietary laws.

JEWISH PRAYER AND WORSHIP

QUESTIONS
1. With which qualities should God be worshipped?
2. Why do we want to be close to God?

3. Formal prayer is marked by three things. What are they?

ANSWERS
1. With honesty, sincerity, joy and gladness.
2. Because He is the absolute of all goodness and righteousness.
3. a) Prayers must be recited with a *minyan* (quorum of ten adult males);
b) They must be recited at a definite time of the day;
c) They are read from a prayerbook (*Siddur*).

4. What is meant by "informal prayer"?

5. a) Can you give the shortest prayer in the Bible (in Hebrew or English)?
b) By whom was it spoken?
c) Why was it said?

6. Which type of prayer is more acceptable to God, formal or informal?

7. Why is an informal prayer not always possible or practical for most of us today?

8. a) What was the "Great Synagogue"?
b) Which famous prayer did its members compose?

9. Why are ten adult Jews necessary for a *minyan?*

10. Why is a *minyan* necessary for a congregation?

11. a) Give the basic meaning of the word "Siddur".
b) Why is it so called?

12. Give the general order of the services followed in almost every *Siddur.*

13. a) What else can you learn from a *Siddur* besides prayer?
b) Give a few examples.

4. Prayers we compose ourselves and recite at any time of our choosing.

5. a) *Kayl, na, refa na lah!* ("O God, please heal her!"
b) Moses.
c) To heal his sister, Miriam, from leprosy.

6. Both are equally acceptable to Him, as long as they are offered with honesty and sincerity.

7. Most of us cannot always express our thoughts or always organize them properly at the right time and the right place.

8. a) A body of 120 scholars who led the religious life of the Jews following the Babylonian Exile.
b) The *Shemoneh Essrei,* or *Amidah.*

9. In the account of the "ten spies" (Num. 14:27) the Bible refers to the ten men as an *edah* (congregation). Hence, it is assumed that a group of ten males is needed to constitute a congregation.

10. Certain prayers can be recited and the Torah reading can be conducted only with a *minyan* present.

11. a) Order.
b) All the prayers are arranged in traditional "order."

12. Morning, afternoon, evening, Sabbath and festival prayers, and miscellaneous other prayers.

13. a) Material for study.
b) Portions from the Torah, Talmud, and other Jewish writings.

14. Name one advantage of having Jewish congregations the world over follow a traditional *Siddur*.

15. Name the three general classes of prayers.

16. Which famous prayer contains all three classes of prayer (as in 15, above)?

17. a) Name the earliest post-Biblical prayer to be written down.
    b) Who composed it?

18. Who set up the earliest order of prayer service, and when?

19. How do the Ashkenazic and Sephardic prayerbooks differ from one another?

20. a) How many times each weekday is each of the following prayers recited?
    Amidah, Shema, Aleinu, Ashrei.
    b) Give the service when each of these is recited.

21. What are the three major ideas in the weekday *Amidah?*

22. How does the middle portion of the *Amidah* differ on weekdays, Sabbaths, and festivals?

23. a) While reciting the *Amidah*, what motions or actions does the worshipper perform?
    b) Why?

14. The uniform *Siddur* enables the Jew to feel at home in whatever synagogue he may find himself.

15. Petition; praise and glorification; and thanksgiving.

16. The *Shemoneh Essrei*, or *Amidah*.

17. a) The *Amidah*.
    b) Ezra and the scholars of the Great Synagogue.

18. Rabbi Amram Gaon of Babylonia, about 850 C.E.

19. In the arrangement and wording of certain prayers and by the addition of certain prayers in the Sephardic *Siddur*.

20. a) Three.
    b) *Amidah:* Shaharit, Minhah, Arvit.
    Shema: Shaharit, Arvit, and at bedtime.
    Aleinu: At the close of each service.
    Ashrei: Shaharit (twice); and at Minhah.

21. Praise, petition, thanksgiving.

22. During weekdays 13 paragraphs of petition are said. On holy days the 13 are substituted by certain others referring to the Sabbath or festivals.

23. a) He stands facing east, prayers in an undertone, and bows at certain points in the service.
    b) He acts as though he were standing before a King.

24. a) Of all the prayers mentioned so far, which is the oldest?
b) From where does it come?

25. Which is the most basic idea of the *Shema?*

26. a) Into how many parts is the *Shema* divided (following the opening lines)?
b) Give the basic thought of each part.

27. Which two basic ideas do we express in the *Aleinu* prayer?

28. a) Why were Jews persecuted centuries ago for reciting the *Aleinu* prayer?
b) To whom did this objectionable passage actually refer?

29. What is the source of the *Ashrei* prayer?

30. Why has the Ashrei become such a prominent prayer in the daily service?

31. About how many blessings can a pious Jew recite on various occasions every day?

32. Explain briefly each of the following prayerbooks:
a) *Maḥzor;* b) *Kinot;* c) *Seliḥot.*

24. a) The *Shema.*
b) Deuteronomy 6:4-9; 11:13-21; Numbers 15:37-41.

25. The Oneness of God.

26. a) Three.
b) Loving God; promises of reward and punishment; remembering God's commandments at all times.

27. a) We thank Him for having made us Jews and enabled us to worship Him alone as King.
b) The hope that some day all the peoples of the earth will recognize God as the only God.

28. a) It was thought that the sentence in this prayer referring to idol-worshippers had been meant as an insult against the Christians.
b) To the idol-worshippers of about the 4th century, C.E.

29. Mostly Psalm 145, which calls on all mankind to glorify God's majesty and stresses His care of all mankind.

30. According to the Talmud (Berakhot 4b) anyone who recites Psalm 145 three times each day is assured of his share in the world to come.

31. About 100.

32. a) *Maḥzor:* The traditional festival prayerbook.
b) *Kinot:* Prayers of sadness for the Fast of *Av.*

32.

c) *Selihot:* Penitential prayers for the various fasts of the year and the period immediately preceding the High Holidays.

33. Name a few values of prayer.

33. a) It brings you closer to God.

b) You get to feel closer to your fellow-Jews when praying together with a congregation.

c) You can gain much knowledge from the *Siddur,* because it contains passages from the Bible and rabbinical literature.

d) Prayer leaves you with a feeling of joy and inspiration.

JEWISH BURIAL AND MOURNING CUSTOMS

QUESTIONS

1. Why should we study the Jewish laws on death and mourning?

2. On what two principles are most of the Jewish burial and mourning customs based?

3. What is done to express our hope that a seriously ill person will recover?

4. a) What do the words "Barukh Dayan emet" mean?

b) When, and by whom, are they recited?

ANSWERS

1. Because death is part of the life cycle and affects all of us at one time or other.

2. a) Showing the necessary honor and respect for the departed.

b) Concering ourselves with the feelings of the survivors and helping and comforting them in every way possible.

3. Psalms and special prayers are read for the patient's recovery.

4. a) "Blessed be the true Judge."

b) They are recited by the survivors at the bedside of the departed, and also on receiving news that someone has died.

5. Describe the "keriah" ritual.

5. All close relatives make a small rent in one of their outer garments; on the left side for parents, on the right side for other relatives.

6. What is the "Ḥevrah Kaddisha"?

6. The "burial society" which attends to the body for burial.

7. a) What type of material is used for a shroud?
   b) Why?

7. a) Plain white linen.
   b) To show that all persons, regardless of their position during life, are equal in death.

8. What is done at home to express the family's grief for the dead?

8. All pictures, mirrors, etc., are covered or put away, and a large candle is left burning for 7 days.

9. a) How soon after the death should a Jewish funeral take place?
   b) Why?

9. a) Usually within 24 hours.
   b) It is considered disrespectful to allow the dead to lie unburied longer than absolutely necessary.

10. What is a "hesped"?

10. A eulogy of the dead. It is usually delivered by a rabbi or a close friend of the deceased.

11. Why is the attendance at a funeral considered to be a *hesed shel emet* (an act of true loving kindness)?

11. Because this is one act of kindness for which one cannot expect a reward.

12. What words are spoken to the mourners at the close of the burial service?

12. "May the Lord comfort you among the other mourners of Zion and Jerusalem."

13. How do friends and neighbors show their kindness to the mourners following the funeral service?

13. They prepare the first full meal for the bereaved family.

14. a) What is the "shiva" period?
    b) What rules must the mourners follow during that period?

14. a) The seven-day period of mourning following the funeral.
    b) They sit on low benches or stools, wear no leather footwear, do no work, and do not leave the house.

15. For the loss of which relatives must a person sit *shiva?*
16. On which days are the rules of *shiva* not to be observed?
17. a) What is meant by the "sheloshim" period?
    b) How does it differ from *shiva?*

18. Give a few restrictions which must be observed during *sheloshim.*

19. How long must mourning continue for parents?
20. How long must the *Kaddish* be recited?
21. Through which observance are the departed remembered permanently?

22. Name a few ways of observing *Yahrzeit.*

23. At what other time, besides the *Yahrzeit*, should the departed be remembered, and how?
24. When should the tombstone be set for the departed?

25. Which central thought or idea is found in the *Kaddish?*

15. Father, mother, wife, husband, son, daughter, brother or sister.
16. On Sabbaths and festivals.
17. a) The thirty-day period of mourning following death.
    b) The mourner may carry on his usual way of life, except for certain restrictions.
18. a) No new clothes are worn.
    b) Men must not shave or have a haircut.
    c) Mourners stay away from public celebrations and entertainments.
    d) Mourners must not marry during that period.
19. For twelve months from the date of death.
20. For eleven months.

21. By the *Yahrzeit* (anniversary of the death), which is observed each year on the anniversary of the death.
22. a) Lighting a memorial candle which is to burn from sundown to sundown.
    b) Attendance at synagogue services by the sons, who recite the *Kaddish.*
    c) Studying Torah.
    d) Donating to some charity.

23. On the last day of the major festivals, when the *Yizkor* prayer is recited.

24. Any time after *sheloshim*, but usually about a year following death.

25. The *Kaddish* makes no mention of death or mourning. It is a proclamation of praise for God's justice and righteousness.

26. When is the *Kaddish* recited other than concerning death?

26. During synagogue services, in a slightly different form, to mark the end or a point of transition in a portion of the service.

27. How does the requirement of a *minyan* for reciting the *Kaddish* help the mourner?

27. In the presence of others the mourner obtains comfort from the feeling that someone else shares his sorrow.

28. In what language is the *Kaddish* written? Why?

28. In Aramaic. This was the everyday language used by the common people at the time the *Kaddish* was composed. The use of Aramaic was intended to make the *Kaddish* understood by all.

29. What is perhaps the best way of honoring the dead?

29. By emulating the noble character traits for which the deceased is best remembered.

THE HEBREW CALENDAR

QUESTIONS

ANSWERS

1. a) What name is given to the calendar commonly in use today?
   b) Why is it called a "solar" calendar?

1. a) Civil calendar.
   b) It is based on the movements of the earth around the *sun*.

2. a) Our Hebrew calendar is also called a _____ calendar.
   b) Why?

2. a) Lunar.
   b) Because it is based on the movements of the *moon* around the earth.

3. a) How many days are there in the solar year?
   b) In the lunar year?
   c) Which is the shorter, and by how many days?
   d) How does this difference affect the time of our festivals?

3. a) 365.
   b) 354.
   c) The lunar, by 11 days.
   d) It makes them come out earlier each year. This is the reason why there are leap years in which an extra month is added to the calendar.

4. Why should it matter to us if our festivals would keep coming out earlier, year after year?

5. a) If 5739 is 1979 in the civil calendar, how can you figure a Jewish year from a civil year?
b) How do you figure a civil year from a Jewish year?
c) Which Jewish year corresponds to the following civil years? 1914, 1789, 1967, 1865, 1492.
d) What is the civil date for the following Jewish years? 5702, 5684, 4892, 5536.
e) The Second Temple was destroyed in the year 70 C.E. What date is that in the Hebrew calendar?

6. a) How many months are there in an ordinary Hebrew year?
b) in a Hebrew leap year?

7. a) What is the average length of a Hebrew month?
b) How many days can there be in a Hebrew month?

8. a) True or False:
The names of our Hebrew months come from the Five Books of Moses.
b) How are our months referred to in the Pentateuch?

9. a) Only one month is mentioned by name in the Pentateuch. Which is it?
b) What is its present name?
c) Why is that month specially mentioned?

4. The festivals would be coming at the wrong time of the year; for instance, Passover, a spring festival, would come in the winter, and Sukkot, a harvest holiday, would come in the summer or spring.

5. a) By adding 3760 to the civil year.
b) By subtracting 3760 from the Jewish year.
c) 1914 — 5674-75; 1789 — 5549-50; 1967 — 5727-28; 1865 — 5625-26; 1492 — 5252-53
d) 5702 — 1941-42; 5684 — 1923-24; 4892 — 1131-32; 5536 — 1775-76
e) 3830.

6. a) 12.
b) 13.

7. a) 29.5 days.
b) 29 or 30 days.

8. a) False: None of our present months are mentioned by their present names in the Pentateuch (Five Books of Moses).
b) By number only.

9. a) *Aviv*, the first month of the Hebrew year.
b) *Nisan*.
c) Because it was the month that marked the beginning of freedom for the Israelites as they left Egypt.

10. a) Name the thirteenth (additional) month of the year.
b) When does it come?

11. In which Books of the Bible are our present Hebrew months first mentioned by their Hebrew names?

12. Where in the Bible do we find the first reference to the number of days in a week?

13. a) In the civil calendar the days of the week are called "Sunday, Monday," etc. How are they referred to in the Bible?
b) Why do we Jews name each day in this way?

14. When does the Jewish day begin?

15. Which terms do we use instead of "B.C. (before Christ)" and "A.D. (Anno Domino)" of the civil calendar?

16. Why was it necessary for our ancestors to determine the first day of each month?

17. a) In ancient Israel how would the first day of each month be determined?
b) How was this information then brought to the people during the earliest times of our history?

18. a) Why did bonfire relays become unsatisfactory?
b) What method of communication was used to replace the bonfires?

10. a) *Adar Sheni* (Second *Adar*).
b) Only during a leap year.

11. Zekhariah, Esther, and Nehemiah.

12. In Genesis 2:2-3, in the story of Creation.

13. a) By number (1st day, 2nd day, 3rd day, etc.) except the 7th day, "Sabbath."
b) Because in this way we count the days as they approach the Sabbath, for which we wait anxiously.

14. At sundown, because we are told in the story of the days of Creation that "there was evening and there was morning" (Genesis 1:5, etc.).

15. B.C.E. — Before the Common Era.
C.E. — During the Common Era.

16. So that they could figure the dates of the various festivals.

17. a) Observers would watch the moon and then report to the Sanhedrin.
b) Through bonfires which would be lit on every hill and relayed to others elsewhere.

18. a) (1) The Samaritans would light bonfires at the wrong time in order to confuse the people.
(2) The danger of fire increased with the growth of population.
b) Messengers would be sent out to inform the people, both in the Holy Land and in other lands.

19. Why do Jews outside of Israel observe an additional day for the festivals?

19. Because the messengers would often be late in reaching the people in outlying areas, and the people were thus left in doubt as to the exact day of the holiday.

20. a) Why did it later become necessary to establish a fixed calendar?
b) Who originated the rules for the first written calendard, and when?

20. a) Bonfires and messengers had become impractical; also, by now, Jews had gained more knowledge of astronomy, thereby enabling them to establish a fixed calendar.
b) Hillel II, about 360 C.E.

21. a) On which days of the week can the first day of Rosh Hashanah never fall?
b) Explain why not, for each day.

21. a) Sunday, Wednesday or Friday.
b) *Sunday:* to prevent Hoshanah Rabbah from falling on Sabbath, when beating the "Hoshanah" leaves is forbidden.
Wednesday, Friday: To keep Yom Kippur from falling on a Friday, when preparing for Sabbath would be impractical, or on a Sunday, which would also be impractical.

22. How do we prevent Rosh Hashanah from falling on the wrong day?

22. By adding an extra day during one year and removing it the following year.

23. How many days, then, are there in a regular year and in a leap year when days are added or subtracted?

23. *Regular year:* 355 when a day is added, or 353 when it is subtracted.
Leap Year: 385 when a day is added, and 383 when it is subtracted.

24. Name the Hebrew months.

24. *Nisan, Iyar, Sivan, Tammuz, Av, Elul, Tishri, Ḥeshvan, Kislev, Tevet, Shvat, Adar, Adar Sheni* (during a leap year).

ROSH ḤODESH

1. a) What does the Torah command us to do to observe Rosh Ḥodesh?
   b) Where is the observance of Rosh Ḥodesh commanded?
2. How does the observance of Rosh Ḥodesh, as commanded in the Torah, differ from that of other festivals commanded there?
3. Give the meaning of the term "Rosh Ḥodesh."
4. Was Rosh Ḥodesh ever observed as a major festival?

5. a) When and where is the coming of Rosh Ḥodesh announced today?
   b) Name the prayer which announces it.

6. a) What is meant by the "Molad"?
   b) Where is its coming announced?

7. What other information is announced in the "Birkhat ha-Ḥodesh" prayer?

8. Fill in the correct numbers in each of the following blanks:
   When the outgoing month contains a)_____ days, Rosh Ḥodesh is to be observed for b)_____ days, that is, on the c)_____ day of the old month, and d) _____ of the new month.

1. a) Announce its coming with the sounding of trumpets and offer special sacrifices.
   b) In the Bible, Numbers 28:11-15.
2. Work is not forbidden on Rosh Ḥodesh.

3. The "Beginning of the month."
4. Probably, in ancient times, for the Bible makes some mention of Rosh Ḥodesh feasts.

5. a) On the Sabbath before Rosh Ḥodesh, during synagogue services.
   b) "Birkhat ha-Ḥodesh," or "The Blessing of the New Moon."

6. a) The exact moment each month when the moon stands between the earth and the sun.
   b) In the Sabbath prayer, "Birkhat ha-Ḥodesh."

7. The name of the new month and the day or days of the coming week when it begins.

8. a) 30; b) 2; c) 30th; d) first; e) 29; f) 1; g) first.

But if the old month contains e)___days, then, f)___ day is observed; the g)___ of the new month. observed today?

10. Name two prayers recited on Rosh Ḥodesh.

9. By special prayers and Torah readings.

10. *Ya'aleh v'Yavo* ("May our prayers arise") in the *Amidah* and the Grace after Meals; Hallel (a selection of psalms of praise); and Musaf (the additional service to commemorate the Rosh Ḥodesh offerings brought in the Temple).

11. a) For which month is the "Blessing of the New Moon" never recited?
b) Why not?

11. a) *Tishri.*
b) Because Rosh Hashanah, the beginning of the New Year, falls on the first day of *Tishri.*

12. What is meant by "Kiddush ha-Levanah" ("Sanctification of the New Moon")?

12. An evening ceremony in which we go outdoors and "welcome" the new moon.

13. When and where does the "Kiddush ha-Levanah" ceremony usually take place?

13. On a Saturday night between the 3rd and 16th of each month, usually outside the synagogue.

14. At the close of which two fasts is the "Kiddush ha-Levanah" ceremony also held?

14. At the close of Yom Kippur and the Fast of Av.

15. How is Rosh Ḥodesh observed in this country, outside of its synagogue observances?

15. By special celebrations and programs.

16. Why has it been proposed that Rosh Ḥodesh be made a national holiday in Israel?

16. So that Israelis, whose only day of rest is the Sabbath, might enjoy an additional "weekend" holiday.

17. What is meant by "Shabbat Mevorakhim"?

17. The Sabbath when the prayer for the New Moon is recited.

18. What special customs do many pious Jewish women observe on Rosh Ḥodesh?

18. They refrain from sewing and from certain other forms of work that can be put off.

19. Name a few additional customs observed for Rosh Hodesh by Jews in some different lands.

19. a) Fasting and reciting penitential prayers (just as for a fast day) on the day before Rosh Hodesh.
b) Wearing new clothes for the first time just as for a major festival.

FOR FURTHER READING

Abrahams, Israel, *Jewish Life in the Middle Ages*
Arian, Phillip, and Eisenberg, Azriel, *The Story of the Prayerbook*
Bermant, Chaim, *The Walled Garden*
Birnbaum, Philip, *A Book of Jewish Concepts*
Cohen, Jacob, *The Royal Table*
Dembitz, L.N., *Jewish Services in Synagogue and Home*
Donin, H.H. *To Be A Jew*
_____, *To Raise a Jewish Child*
Edidin, Ben, *Jewish Customs and Ceremonies*
Eisenberg, Azriel, *The Story of the Jewish Calendar*
_____, *The Synagogue Through the Ages*
Epstein, Louis M., *The Jewish Marriage Contract*
Epstein, Morris, *All About Jewish Holidays and Customs*
Freedman, Seymour, *The Book of Kashruth*
Friedlander, M., *The Jewish Religion*
Garfiel, Evelyn, *Service of the Heart*
Goldin, Hyman, *Code of Jewish Law*
Golomb, Morris, *Know Your Festivals and Enjoy Them*
Goodman, P. and A., *The Marriage Anthology*
Gottlieb, Nathan, *A Jewish Child Is Born*
Grunfeld, I., *The Jewish Dietary Laws* (2 Vols.)
Hertz, J.H., *The Authorized Daily Prayerbook*
Hertz, J.H., *The Pentateuch and the Haftorahs*
Hirsch, S.M., *Timeless Torah*
Idelsohn, A.Z., *Ceremonies of Judaism*
Jacobs, Louis, *Jewish Prayer*
Kitov, A.E., *The Book of Our Heritage* (3 Vols.)
_____, *The Jew and His Home*
Kolatch, A.J., *The Name Dictionary*
Kon, A., *Prayer*
Lamm, Maurice, *The Jewish Way in Death and Mourning*
Litwin, B., *The Sanctity of the Synagogue*
Mindel, N., *My Prayer*
Routhenberg, L.S., and Seldin, P.R., *The Jewish Wedding Book*
Schauss, Hayyim, *The Lifetime of a Jew*
Speier, Arthur, *The Comprehensive Jewish Calendar*
Sperling, I., *Reasons for Jewish Customs and Traditions*
Sussman, A. and Segal, A., *A Guide for Jewish Youth*
Vitry, S., *Mahzor Vitry*
Zeligs, D., *The Story of Jewish Holidays and Customs*

GLOSSARY

Aaron — The older brother of Moses, who became the first High Priest.

Abel — The second son of Adam and Eve.

Abraham — The first Hebrew to have believed in God.

Additional Service — See MUSAF.

Aleinu — A famous ancient prayer recited at the close of each of the three daily services confirming our belief that God alone is our King, and the only one to be worshipped.

Aliyah — The honor of being called up to the Torah while it is read on weekdays, Sabbaths, or festivals.

Altar — A place, especially a raised platform, where sacrifices or offerings used to be made for religious purposes in ancient times.

Amen — The response to a blessing, indicating agreement with what was said in the blessing.

Am ha-Aretz — A Hebrew term referring to one ignorant of Jewish learning.

Amidah ("standing") — Also known as SHEMONEH ESSREI. A prayer containing nineteen blessings, recited three times daily, with fewer blessings on Sabbath and festivals.

Amram Gaon — A famous Gaon, who lived during the 9th century C.E., and who is best known for having composed the first framework of the present-day Siddur.

Amud — A reading desk used in the synagogue from which some of the prayer services are chanted.

Aramaic — A language akin to Hebrew used in some prayers and many Jewish writings.

Ark, Holy — See ARON HA-KODESH.

Aron ha-Kodesh ("Holy Ark") — A cabinet, or place in the synagogue, where the Torah Scrolls are kept.

Arvit (also called MA'ARIV) — The third of the three required prayers, recited daily after nightfall.

Ashkenazic — Usually refers to the Jews of Europe, especially with regard to their style of prayer services and their manner of pronunciation of Hebrew.

Ashrei — One of the daily prayers recited twice in the morning and once in the afternoon, arranged in alphabetical order.

Aufruf — The "calling up" of a bridegroom for an Aliyah (Torah honor) on the Sabbath prior to his wedding.

Avelut ("Mourning") — Refers to the first year following death, when the survivors observe a period of mourning.

206

Aviv ("Ripening") — Refers to the month of Nisan, the month when the Israelites left Egypt.

Ba'al Korei — The "Torah reader" who reads the Torah portion on weekdays, Sabbaths, and festivals.

Babylonia — The land to which the Jews were exiled following the destruction of the First Temple (586 B.C.E.) and which later served as a noted center of Jewish learning.

Bar Mitzvah, Bat Mitzvah — The act of a Jewish boy reaching the age of 13 years plus one day, and a Jewish girl, 12 years plus one day, when he or she becomes a Jewish adult and is from then on responsible for observing the commandments of the Torah as they apply to each of them.

B.C.E. "Before the Common Era" — Used in place of B.C.

Beged ("Garment") — Refers to the cloth portion of a tallit, to which the tzitzit are attached.

Bet Din — A rabbinical court.

Bet ha-Knesset ("House of Assembly") — A common name given to a synagogue indicating its function as a meeting place as well as a place of worship.

Bet ha-Midrash ("House of Study") — Another name given to a synagogue, where study also takes place.

Bet Tefillah ("House of Prayer") — A name indicating that a synagogue functions as a place of worship.

Bible — The Torah, consisting of the Law (Torah), the works of the Prophets, and the Holy Writings, together called the "Tanakh."

Bimah ("Pulpit," "platform") — The place which is traditionally set apart from the Aron ha-Kodesh in the synagogue.

Birkhat ha-Ḥodesh ("Blessing of the month") — The prayer recited on the Sabbath before the beginning of a Hebrew month.

Blessing of the New Moon — See BIRKHAT HA-ḤODESH.

Book of Esther — One of the best-known of the Five Scrolls (Megillot), where the story of Purim is told.

Brit Milah — See COVENANT OF CIRCUMCISION.

Cain — The oldest son of Adam and Eve.

Canaan — The ancient name for Israel during early Biblical times.

Cantor (Ḥazzan, in Hebrew) — The man who chants the prayers of the synagogue services.

Caro, Joseph — The editor of the Shulḥan Arukh, in the 15th century.

C.E. — "Common Era" — a term used in place of A.D.

Chair of Elijah — The special chair used at a circumcision ceremony.

Circumcision — A ceremony consisting of a minor operation on a Jewish male infant on the 8th day after birth.

Confessional Prayer — The prayer of confession recited on Yom Kippur, every line beginning with the words "Al Ḥayt" ("for the sins of . . .").

Covenant of Circumcision — A commandment which applies to every Jewish male on the eighth day of his life as a sign of the Covenant made between God and Abraham.

David — The noted warrior and second king of Israel who united the Twelve Tribes into one kingdom. Also famous for his writings.

Deuteronomy — The fifth of the Five Books of Moses.

Dietary Laws — The laws of Kashrut which deal with food that is permitted or forbidden.

Eben ha-Ezer — The section of the Shulḥan Arukh which deals with family matters, including marriage and divorce.

Eighteen Blessings — See SHEMONEH ESSREI.

Erev Pesaḥ — The day before Passover.

Etrog — The citrus fruit that is used during the festival of Sukkot.

Exodus — The departure of the Israelites from Egypt, under the leadership of Moses.

Ezekiel — The third of the three Major Prophets.

Ezra — The famous scribe who returned to Israel from Babylonia during the 5th century B.C.E., to reconstruct the religious life of the Jews.

Ezrat Nashim ("Court of the Women") — Originally, the women's section in the Temple. Today, it refers to the women's section in an Orthodox synagogue.

Fast of Av — The Major Fast that is observed on the ninth day of the month of Av, in commemoration of the destruction of both Temples and of other sad events in the history of our people.

Fast of Gedaliah — A minor fast observed on the day following Rosh Hashanah, in memory of the murder of Gedaliah, a popular Jewish governor, following the destruction of the First Temple.

First Temple — The Temple in Jerusalem, built by King Solomon, and destroyed by the Babylonians in 586 B.C.E.

Five Scrolls — Five short books in the Holy Writings which are read on various festivals and fasts during the year.

Gabbai — The head officer during synagogue services.

Gaon (pl. *Geonim*) — The Jewish scholars in Babylonia who were regarded as the leaders of Jewish religious life during the period of about 600 — 1000 C.E.

Gemara — The second basic section of the Talmud, which is an explanation of the Mishnah.

Get — Hebrew for a Jewish Divorce.

Golden Calf — The object of worship of the Israelites who sinned during Moses' absence while on Mount Sinai.

Grace After Meals (Birkhat ha-Mazon) — The prayer of thanks recited following a meal where bread has been eaten.

Great Synagogue — A body of 120 famous scholars who guided the political and religious life of the Jews during the 5th century B.C.E.

Gregorian Calendar — The civil calendar in common use today, established by Pope Gregory XIII in 1583.

Half Hallel — The abridged version of the Hallel prayer, recited on Rosh Hodesh and the last six days of Passover.

Hallel — A prayer of thanksgiving recited on Rosh Hodesh. Hanukah, Passover, Shavuot, and Sukkot.

Hametz ("Leaven" or, that which ferments) — Bread or other "leavened" food that may not be eaten, used or owned during Passover.

Hanukkah — A minor festival, commemorating the rededication of the Second Temple on the 25th of Kislev, 165 B.C.E.

Havdalah ("Separation") — The prayer recited at the close of the Sabbath and festivals to indicate that work forbidden on a holy day may now be resumed.

Hebrew Day School — A school where both Hebrew and general studies are taught during normal school hours.

Hevra Kaddisha ("Sacred Society") — An organization that takes charge of preparing a dead body for burial, according to Jewish law.

Hezekiah — A famous king of the kingdom of Judah, who lived during the 8th century B.C.E., noted for his struggle for the true worship of God, instead of idolatry.

High Priest — The KOHEN GADOL who served as head of the Temple in conducting the various sacrifices and offerings.

Hillel — The famous scholar who lived around the 1st century B.C.E. and one of the most outstanding rabbis in the Mishneh.

Hillel II — A famous scholar who lived around 360 C.E., and established certain rules which form the basis of our present-day Hebrew calendar.

Hol ha-Moed — (The "weekday portion of the festival") — The middle four days of Passover and Sukkot, — a "half-holiday."

Hoshana Rabbah — The seventh day of Sukkot when the worshippers, carrying an Etrog and Lulav, march around the Bimah in the synagogue chanting the Hoshana prayers.

Hoshen Mishpat — The section of the Shulhan Arukh which deals with civil and criminal law.

Hulin — The tractate of the Talmud containing most of the laws of ritual slaughter.

Humash — Hebrew for the Five Books of Moses, or, the Pentateuch.

Huppah — The bridal canopy under which a married couple stand during the wedding ceremony.

Hyrcanus, Eliezer Ben — One of the most outstanding scholars of the Mishneh, who lived around the 1st century B.C.E.

Isaac — The son of Abraham and Sarah, and second of the Three Patriarchs.

Jacob — The son of Isaac and Rebbekah, and the third of the Three Patriarchs.

Joshua Ben Hananiah — One of the outstanding tannaim (authors of the Mishnah) who lived during the 1st-2nd centuries C.E., and who is also known for the great help he gave to the Jews when they were in trouble.

Joshua Bin Nun — The leader of the Israelites following the death of Moses.

Kabalah — A certificate or license granted to a shoḥet permitting him to practice Sheḥitah (ritual slaughtering).

Kaddish — An ancient prayer recited in the synagogue at the conclusion of a portion of the service either by the cantor or by a mourner.

Kasher ("To make something kosher") — Usually refers to the making of cooking utensils and vessels fit for Passover, or other, use.

Kashrut (Laws of), ("Dietary Laws") — Those rules and regulations that determine the food that we eat.

Kedushah ("Sanctification") — A prayer recited (only in the presence of a minyan) during the Shemoneh Essrei prayer.

Keriah — The tearing of the garments by the kin of a deceased, as a sign of grief.

Ketubah — The marriage contract, read during a wedding ceremony.

Kiddush — A prayer of sanctification recited on Sabbath and festivals over wine.

Kiddush ha-Levanah ("Sanctification of the new moon") — A ceremony observed on a Saturday night between the 3rd and 16th of most months, with a minyan, in the courtyard of the synagogue, before a visible moon, when certain special prayers are recited.

King Solomon — King of Israel, son of David, best-known for having built the First Temple and also as the author of certain Biblical writings.

Kippah — See YARMULKE.

Kohen (pl. *Kohanim*) — A descendant of the Kohanim, the Priests in the Temple at Jerusalem.

Kosher L'Pesaḥ — Any food or other item which is permitted for Passover use.

Lag B'Omer — The 33rd day of the "Counting of the Omer" which serves as a break in the period of semi-mourning (in memory of the deaths of the students of Rabbi Akiva during the 2nd century C.E.), when joyous events, formerly prohibited, are again permitted.

Lamdan — A person who is well-learned in Jewish lore, especially in Talmudic studies.

Leap Year, Jewish — A year when a month is added to the 12 regular months every two or three years.

Levi, Levite — A descendant of the Levites, who used to assist the Kohanim (the Priests) in the service of the ancient Temple.

Leviticus — The third of the Five Books of Moses, including laws of sacrifices, purity, the festivals, clean and unclean foods, and other matters.

Lishkat ha-Gazit ("Court of Hewn Stone") — The place in the Second Temple where the Sanhedrin used to meet.

Luaḥ ("Calendar") — Hebrew for a printed Hebrew calendar.

Lulav — The palm branch used during the festival of Sukkot.

Lunar Calendar — A calendar based on the movements of the moon, which is the one Jews observe.

Ma'ariv — See ARVIT.

Maccabeans — The sons of Mattathias, noted as the heroes of the story of Ḥanukah.

Magen David ("Shield of David") — A six-pointed emblem used in Jewish decorations in the synagogue and elsewhere.

Maḥzor — A special festival prayerbook.

Maḥzor Vitry — A famous Maḥzor composed by Simḥa of Vitry, during the 12th century C.E., and which contains much material used in other prayerbooks ever since.

Maimonides, Moses — The renowned scholar, rabbi and physician, who lived in Spain and Egypt, between 1135 and 1204.

Major Fast — A fast (such as Yom Kippur) which lasts from evening to evening.

Major Festival — A festival that is commanded in the Torah (the Pentateuch), when all work is forbidden.

Mashgiaḥ ("Supervisor," "Inspector") — One who performs religious supervision, especially for the observance of Kashrut.

Matzah Shemurah — "Matzah that is specially guarded" from the time the wheat is harvested.

Megillah — ("A small hand-written scroll") — A term generally referring to one of the Five Scrolls of the Bible, usually to the Megillah of Esther.

Meḥitzah — The divider found in Orthodox congregations which separates the women's section from that of the men's.

Mezumen — A minimum of three adult male Jews, who are permitted to recite the Grace after Meals as a group.

Mezuzah — A small piece of parchment enclosed in a case and which contains the Biblical commandment to place a mezuzah on the doorpost of one's house.

Middle Ages — That period of world history which began with the fall of the Roman Empire (about 476 C.E.) and which lasted until the Modern Period, beginning around 1500-1600.

Midrash — Those holy books which seek to find new and mysterious meaning for the verses in the Bible, through the use of tales, proverbs, and anecdotes.

Mikdash Me'at ("A small sanctuary") — A term often applied to a synagogue.

Minhah — The second of the three required daily prayers, recited during the afternoon.

Minor Fast — A fast lasting from sunrise to sunset (but never on a Sabbath), commemorating some sad event in Jewish history.

Minor Festival — A festival not mentioned in the Pentateuch, as well as Rosh Hodesh, when work is permitted.

Minyan — A group of ten adult Jews, the minimum necessary for synagogue worship.

Miriam — Sister of Moses.

Mishnah — The first basic section of the Talmud.

Mitzvah (pl. *Mitzvot*) — A pious act or deed. A commandment of the Torah.

Mohel — A ritual surgeon, who performs a circumcision operation.

Molad — The exact moment when the new month begins.

(El) Molei Rahamim — The memorial prayer recited in memory of a deceased.

Moses — The leader of the Israelites as they left Egypt and wandered through the desert.

Musaf — The Additional Service, consisting of an additional Amidah, which is recited on Sabbaths and festivals as a reminder of the additional sacrifices offered in the Temple.

Nehemiah — The governor of Judea who came from Persia to Judea to work with Ezra to reestablish the political and religious life of the Jews during the 5th century, B.C.E.

Neilah — The closing prayer of the Yom Kippur service which is recited following the Minha service.

Ner Tamid ("The eternal light") — The light found above the Holy Ark in the synagogue.

Nisan — The first of the Hebrew months, when Passover falls.

Noah — The righteous man who was saved from the Great Flood by building an Ark for his family and certain living creatures.

Numbers, Book of — The fourth of the Five Books of Moses, containing historical material regarding the Israelites' forty-year wanderings in the desert.

Orah Hayyim — The first of the four sections of the Shulhan Arukh, which deals with daily conduct, prayers, holidays, etc.

Oral Law — That body of laws which explains the Written Law (Torah); the Talmud.

Paschal Lamb — The special Passover offering, as commanded in Exodus, 12.

Passover — The festival commemorating the Exodus of the Israelites from Egyptian slavery, under the leadership of Moses.

Pasul — Anything that is forbidden or unfit to be used, according to Jewish law, usually referring to non-food items.

Patriarchs — The earliest fathers of the Jewish people — Abraham, Isaac, and Jacob.

Penitential Prayers, ("Seliḥot" in Hebrew) — A set of prayers asking divine forgiveness of sins, recited on Yom Kippur, Fast Days, and during certain other services.

Pidyon ha-Ben — Hebrew for "Redeeming of the First-Born (son)."

Priestly Blessing — The ceremony of the Kohanim blessing the congregation during festivals.

Prophet — A person who, during Biblical times, could communicate with God and report His message to the people in terms they could understand.

Psalms, Book of — One of the books of Holy Writings, containing 150 poems.

Purim — A famous minor festival commemorating the miracle of the salvation of the Jews of Persia from the wicked plot of Haman to destroy them.

Pushke — A Yiddish term for a money box used for collecting coins for charitable purposes.

Qwatter — The godfather, who hands the infant to be circumcised to the Mohel.

Rabbi, Rav — The title given to an ordained Hebrew scholar, many of whom serve as spiritual leader of a congregation.

Rachel — One of the wives of Jacob, the third of the three Patriarchs.

Rashi — (Hebrew abbreviation of Rabbi Shlomo Yitzḥaki, who lived from 1040 to 1105) — Famous Biblical commentator, best-known for his clear and simple style of interpretations.

Responsa — Answers to questions on Jewish law and observances as given by rabbinic scholars in reply to inquiries addressed to them.

Retzuah — A strap fastened to each of the tefillin cases.

Rosh Hashanah — The festival which ushers in the New Year on the first two days of Tishri, when the Shofar is sounded during services.

Rosh Ḥodesh — A half-holiday observed during the first day or two of every Hebrew month (except Tishri) to mark the beginning of the month.

Sabbath — The seventh day of the week, when no work is permitted, as commanded in the Torah.

Samaritans — A people living in Israel during the days of the Second Temple who became unfriendly to the Jews.

Sandek — The godfather, who holds the male infant during the circumcision ceremony.

Sanhedrin — A body of 71 learned scholars which served, during the period of the Talmud, both as a Supreme Court and as a law-making body.

Scribe — See SOFER.

Second Temple — The Temple in Jerusalem, built by the returning exiles from Babylonia, and destroyed by the Romans in 70 C.E.

Seder ("Order") — The special home service held on the first two nights of Passover.

Sefirah ("Counting") — The days of the Omer counting period (between Passover and Shavuot) which are observed as days of partial mourning.

Selihot — See PENITENTIAL PRAYERS.

Semikhah ("Ordination") — The act of permitting a man to be admitted to the rabbinate.

Sephardic — Pertaining to the religious practices of the Jews of southern Europe and the Middle East, also, to their prayer style and pronunciation of Hebrew.

Shaddai — (Usually, "God Almighty," one of the names by which Jews refer to God). The word formed while putting on the tefillin shel rosh and shel yad.

Shaharit — The morning service.

Shaliah — A "messenger," who delivers a "Get" (divorce document) to one party to a divorce in behalf of the other party.

Shaliah Tzibbur ("the congregation's representative") — Another term for "CANTOR."

Shalom Bayit ("Peace in the Home") — An expression describing a quiet, harmonious, and peaceful home.

Shalom Zakhor — A special celebration observed in honor of a male infant on the Sabbath before his circumcision.

Shammash — The "sexton," or the person who attends to the care of the religious articles used in the synagogue (Siddurim, Humashim, etc.) as well as to other needs around the synagogue.

Shavuot ("Feast of Weeks") — A two-day major Festival which comes seven weeks after Passover; the day when the Torah was given on Mt. Sinai and when the Bikkurim used to be offered.

Sheloshim — The "thirty day" period of mourning following death.

Shel Rosh ("Of the Head") — The tefillin case containing four parchments, and which is worn on the head.

Shel Yad ("Of the hand") — The tefillin case containing the single parchment that is worn on the left hand.

Shema (Prayer) — The prayer recited thrice daily declaring God's unity.

Shemini Atzeret (Eighth day of Solemn Assembly) — The festival following the seven days of Sukkot.

Shemoneh Essrei (The "Eighteen Blessings" also known as "Amidah") — The central prayer, recited three times daily, in a standing position.

Sheva Berakhot — The "Seven Blessings" recited during a marriage ceremony.

Shin — The Hebrew letter that is engraved on the side of the shel rosh. It is also the shape of the letter formed on the back of the hand of the tefillin shel yad.

Shiva — The "seven day" period of deep mourning that begins immediately following the burial of the deceased.

Shohet ("Slaughterer") — One who is trained and certified to perform ritual slaughter.

Shulhan ("Table") — The "table" on which the Torah is placed when read and from which the cantor leads the service.

Shulhan Arukh ("A set table") — The authoritative code of Jewish laws, prepared by Joseph Caro during the 15th century.

Siddur — A Hebrew prayerbook.

Sidrah — The section of the Pentateuch that is read in the synagogue every Sabbath.

Simhah Shel Mitzvah — Refers to the joy present while performing a mitzvah (a pious act).

Simhat Torah (Joy in the Torah) — The very last of the Sukkot festivals which celebrates the completion and beginning of the annual Torah reading cycle.

Siyyum ha-Torah — A celebration which marks the completion of the study of some holy book.

Sofer — A Hebrew scribe, one who prepares a Torah scroll, tefillin, mezuzah, divorce document, and others.

Solar Calendar — The civil calendar in common use, which is based on the movements of the earth around the sun.

Spice Box — A box of spices used as part of the Havdalah ceremony at the close of the Sabbath.

Sukkah — A booth or hut, used on the festival of Sukkot as a reminder of God's protection of the Israelites during their desert wanderings.

Sukkot — The Feast of Tabernacles and the third of the Three Festivals of Rejoicing, observed by "dwelling" in a Sukkah and by taking an Etrog and Lulav.

Synagogue — A Jewish place of worship.

Tabernacle — The portable sanctuary carried by the Israelites in their desert wanderings from Egypt to Israel.

Tahanun — A prayer of forgiveness, recited daily except on Sabbath, festivals, and other days of special joy.

Tallit — A prayer shawl containing four fringes, worn by men during prayers.

Tallit Katan ("A small tallit") — A small tzitzit garment worn beneath the shirt.

Talmud — The Oral Law, consisting of the Mishnah and the Gemara.

Talmud Torah — Literally, "the study of Jewish knowledge" but today it usually refers to an afternoon Hebrew school.

Tanakh — A word formed from the initial Hebrew letters "Tav," "Nun," and "Khaf," referring to the Bible as a whole.

Tefillah — The Hebrew term for "prayer." Also refers to the Amidah prayer.

Tefillin ("Phylacteries") — Two black boxes, each containing four chapters from the Bible, hand-written on parchment, with leather straps attached, worn by adult Jewish males during weekday prayer services.

Tehillim — The Book of Psalms, many of which are part of our daily prayers.

Temple — The central sanctuary, located in Jerusalem, and the only place where animal or other sacrifices could be offered.

Tenaim — The "conditions" or "terms" of a marriage as mentioned in the Ketubah. Also, the special betrothal ceremony often held at some time prior to the wedding.

Tisha B'Av ("Ninth of Av") — The sad day of national mourning in memory of the destruction of both the First and Second Temples in Jerusalem. A Major Fast day.

Tishri — The seventh month of the Hebrew calendar, when the High Holidays and the Sukkot festivals come.

Torah — A Torah scroll; the Bible; the Pentatuech (Five Books of Moses); Jewish learning.

Trafe — Food that is forbidden to be eaten because of its not being kosher.

Trop — The musical accent signs that are used for the reading of the Torah.

Tzedakah ("Righteousness," "justice") — Also refers to "charity," "kindness."

Tzitzit ("Fringes") — The four fringes on the corners of a tallit.

Va'ad ha-Kashrut ("A Kashrut organization") — An organization that supervises the preparation and distribution of kosher meat in a Jewish community.

Viduy (Before death) — A special prayer recited by someone close to death.

Wachtnacht ("Watch night") — An ancient custom of "watching" a Jewish child on the eve of his circumcision, to protect him from the evil spirits.

Written Law — Refers to the Torah, as given by God to Moses.

Ya'aleh v'Yavo — The first two important words of a prayer inserted into the Amidah prayer and the Grace after Meals during New Moon and certain festivals.

Yad ("Hand") — The silver pointer used for following the Torah reading by its reader.

Yahrzeit — The anniversary of one's death, that is observed every year, according to the Hebrew calendar date.

Yarmulke — Yiddish word for kippah, or skullcap.

Yihud ("Privacy") — The ceremony of a bride and groom entering a private room immediately following their wedding ceremony for a short period of privacy together.

Yom Kippur ("Day of Atonement") — The Major Fast day, on the 10th of Tishri, observed by a full fast, prayers, and confession of sins.

Yoreh Deah — One of the four sections of the Shulhan Arukh, which includes the Dietary Laws, among others.

INDEX

Shaliaḥ. See Messenger

Shalom Bayit (domestic peace), achieving it, 112-113, 115

Shalom Zakhor (ceremony) 11

Shammash. See Sexton

Shavuot (Feast of Weeks) 79, 131, 143, 162

Shehitah. See Slaughtering

Sheloshim (period) 144; permitted and forbidden practices, 140-141

Shema (prayer) 31, 52, 59, 122, 126-128, 131, 137; Biblical origin, 126-128; content, 126-128; significance, 121, 126

Shemoneh Essrei (prayer). See Amidah

Shivah (period), observances during, 140

Shohet (ritual slaughterer) 91, 92-94, 96; examination following slaughtering, 93; skill in slaughtering, 93; qualifications, 92-93

Shulḥan Arukh (Jewish Code of Laws) 27

Siddur (Hebrew prayerbook) 28, 108, 118, 121, 123, 124, 134; composition of, 120-121; defined, 121; development of, 122-124; forms of prayerbooks, 131-132; origin of, 122; special prayers and blessings, 131; understanding prayers, 134; variations of, 124

Siyyum ha-Torah 16

Slaughtering, humaneness in, 93; hunting forbidden, 93; of fowls, 98-99; of meat, 93; shohet's skill in, 93

Sofer. See Scribe

Solar (sun) Year, length of, 148, 153; and leap year, 149; and lunar year, 148

Soviet Union, circumcision in, 10

Sukkot (Tabernacles) 50, 59, 79, 90, 131, 132, 149, 155, 160

Synagogue 32, 84, 90, 121, 123, 162; and Jewish survival, 76; as a Jewish home, 55-56; attendance at, 73; behavior in, 73-74; defined, 56; financial support of, 72; for unity before God, 74; and prayer, 34; history of, 58-60, 122; influence upon others, 75; membership in a, 72-73, 112; organization of, 70-71; personnel of, 67-69; ritual items, 61-63; the 3 branches of, 60, 61; three-fold character of, 56, 74; why necessary, 57-58, 74; women's section of, 63-64; you and the, 74-76

Syria, 10, 160

Tallit (prayer shawl), Talliyot 40, 41, 43, 70, 90, 138; as a uniform, 45; not for women, 46-47; putting on, 45-46, 51-52; wearing of, 45-46, 50-52; why worn, 46, 47-48

Tallit and Tefillin (combined) 38, 40, 41, 42, 43, 109, 122, 124

Tallit Katan 48, 51

Talmud 19, 29, 32, 87, 108, 121, 134; contents of, 26-27; Kashrut explained in, 90, 93; required of a rabbi, 67-68; studied during Holocaust, 24; studied instead of fasting, 16; studied in synagogue, 60, 66; values in studying, 35. See also Gemara, Mishnah, Oral Law

Tanakh (Bible) 32

Tefillin 43, 45-54, 90, 127; and Bar Mitzvah, 40, 41, 50; care of, 52; contents of, 46; hand, 46, 50, 52; head, 46, 48, 50-51, 52; not for women, 46-47; significance of, 45, 50; use of, 50; when worn, 45, 50; why worn, 46

Temple 61, 86, 104, 120, 122, 123, 126, 132, 154, 155, 162; First, 39, 58, 59, 122, 154; Second, 59, 60

Tenaim (betrothal) 83

Tisha b'Av (Ninth of Av). See Fast of Av.

Tombstone, Unveiling 143-144

Torah 30, 37, 45, 58, 67, 69, 87, 132, 162; as beginning of early education, 110-111; as Jewish tradition, 34; as a source of prayer, 118; calendar unmentioned in, 152; contents of, 25 ff.; definition of, 19; family life and, 110; Pidyon ha-Ben and, 116; pride in, 53; scroll of the, 39, 61, 70, 90; significance of, 21; tallit and tefillin, 46-48. See also Bible, Five Books of Moses, Pentateuch, Torah Study

Torah reading 66, 123, 142, 156, 160, 163; earliest development of, 21, 59; groom called up during, 80, 84; minyan required for, 57, 74, 120; respect for elders during, 110; special portion for Rosh Ḥodesh, 156, during midweek, 64-65

Torah study 13, 21-22, 123; attitudes toward, 22; by adults, 19, 22 ff.; contents of, 19, 24-28; under hardship, 24; values of, 19-22, 35-36. See also Jewish Education

Trafe 91, 93, 96, 98

DATE DUE			